INNER PEACE

AN INTERNAL FAMILY SYSTEMS CHRISTIAN DEVOTIONAL

DONNA GLASER, LPC

Abundant Life Services LLC

Copyright © 2022 by Donna Glaser

All rights reserved.

This book is licensed for your personal enjoyment only. If you're reading this book and did not purchase it, or it was not purchased for your use only, then please return to amazon.com and purchase your own copy. Thank you for respecting the hard work of this author.

Praise for *Inner Peace:*

An Internal Family Systems Christian Devotional

Donna Glaser has gifted readers with gentle guidance for awakening to our true Selves–the drop of the Divine within each of us. *Inner Peace: An Internal Family Systems Christian Devotional* facilitates a true welcoming of each of our parts through reflection on scripture. It is a lovely adjunct either for those new to IFS or new to Christianity.

~ Michelle Glass, CIFSP, author of *Daily Parts Meditation Practice™: A Journey of Embodied Integration for Clients and Therapists*

Donna Glaser's book, *Inner Peace: An Internal Family Systems Christian Devotional*, is an excellent daily reflection companion for anyone but especially for practicing Christians on their walk toward greater Self understanding and healing. In this book, Donna not only beautifully writes about the core principles of the IFS Model but also relates the IFS premises with biblical scripture. Most importantly, she helps to demystify the nature of the human psyche and reclaim words like "meditation" and "looking within" for people of Christian faith.

~ Chris Burris, LMFT, Senior Lead Trainer for the IFS Institute, author of *Creating Healing Circles: Using the Internal Family Systems Model in Facilitating Groups*

Inner Peace: An Internal Family Systems Christian Devotional is an engaging and grace-filled book. With her down-to-earth approach, Donna Glaser seamlessly integrates the Internal Family Systems model with Christian scriptures and Christian thought. She opens a path for befriending parts and facilitates healing relationships between God, ourselves, and every part of our innermost being. *Inner Peace* is a valuable and welcome contribution to the body of work exploring connections between the Christian faith and Internal Family Systems.

~ Mary Steege, author of The Spirit-Led Life: A Christian Encounter with Internal Family Systems.

CONTENTS

	FORWARD	1
1.	Learning About Your Parts	9
2.	I Have Parts?	11
3.	All Parts Are Welcome	15
4.	Three-In-One	17
5.	Namaste, Parts	21
6.	In the Beginning	23
7.	Stuck	27
8.	The Great Flood	29
9.	So Tired	31
10.	Painprints	33
11.	Polar Opposites	35
12.	Big Jobs	39
13.	Ignore Them at Your Peril	41
14.	The Best Me	43
15.	Unlikely Heroes	45
16.	Do You See What I See?	49
17.	The First Step	51
18.	Sitting on the Ash Heap	53
19.	Tell Me Where It Hurts	55

20.	In This Corner...	57
21.	Mean Parts	59
22.	Laugh 'til It Hurts	61
23.	Shame, Shame, Go Away	63
24.	Mirror, Mirror	67
25.	Know and Be Known	69
26.	No Sleep For You!	71
27.	Back to the Present	73
28.	Behind the Wall	75
29.	Negative Reinforcement	77
30.	Exiles Re[peat] [pair] [deem] Relationships	79
31.	Resentment Is A Clue	81
32.	None So Blind	85
33.	Peace At All Cost	87
34.	Perfectly Perfect In Every Way	89
35.	Legacies	91
36.	Time Doesn't Heal	93
37.	The Good, The Bad, & The Ugly	95
38.	Busy, Busy, Busy	97
39.	The Scariest of Them All	99
40.	Leave Before You're Left	101
41.	The Ones We Have to Hate	103
42.	Leave the Past In the Past	105
43.	Fatally Damaged, Permanently Broken	107
44.	Manager Fears	109
45.	Members of the Body	111

46.	Blended, Not Stirred	115
47.	By God's Design	117
48.	Suffer Together	119
49.	Open Hearts	121
50.	It Happened	123
51.	Martha, Martha, Martha	127
52.	Risky Business	131
53.	Freely Given	135
54.	J.O.Y.	137
55.	Different Places on the Path	139
56.	I Believe! Kinda	143
57.	A Heart, Divided	145
58.	Direct Access	147
59.	The Dark	149
60.	Stuck & Confused	151
61.	Leaves the Ninety-Nine	155
62.	Civil War	157
63.	Spiritual Managers	161
64.	Weary & Burdened	163
65.	Jesus Wept	165
66.	Waste Not	169

FORWARD

I promised myself: never again. Why can't I stop?

I'm so lonely. So why do I keep pushing people away?

Once this next project is done, life will finally calm down.

Sound familiar?

Every day is jammed with things to do, projects to finish, and people to take care of. Every night, a battle between exhaustion and feeling guilty about what was left undone. We want to do better. We keep *trying* to do better, but when we can't, we are forced to settle for just keeping up. The world feels chaotic and under attack, yet each day we trudge forward hoping to eventually reach a place where we can rest. Peace of mind (and heart) seems tantalizingly out of reach, lingering just over the horizon of whatever the current goal or crisis is.

You can't wait for life to bring you peace. That's not where peace comes from. Peace comes from God, and it is found inside your own heart. Inside yourself.

In truth, much of the chaos that robs us of peace comes from our own minds, not from the outside world. We spend a lot of our already meager supply of energy stuffing feelings down, burying the past, resisting cravings, running from conflict, or blocking anxious thoughts. Resistance to emotional pain becomes a way of living—an exhausting, discouraging, fruitlessly empty way of living

What happened to the full life we are promised in John 10:10? Or the Fruits of the Spirit? Shouldn't Christians have an easier time trying to access that center of peace that Jesus left with us?

Yes and no. Being Christian doesn't mean we can bypass our emotional pain. We still have to do the difficult and courageous work of looking deep inside, learning to understand our reactions to hurts, past and present, so that we can bring them to God for healing.

You can't heal what you won't face.

Internal Family Systems[SM] is an evidence-based therapeutic approach to understanding and making peace with that inner world. Learning how our parts inside operate—the aspects of our inner world that are responsible for the stuffing, burying, resisting, etc.—will open your heart, allowing you to settle into the quiet peace that has been waiting for you, just beyond the chaos of your mind. Internal Family Systems[SM] (IFS) emphasizes introspection, self-compassion and self-acceptance, and healing for the parts of you that experience intense fear, sadness, and pain.

When you learn how to care for and nurture the deepest, darkest parts of yourself, you will feel the true, abiding power of inner peace. Being at peace within yourself changes your view of yourself, relationships, the world, and, most importantly, opens your heart to receive God's love and grace.

This is the peace you have been yearning for.

Sitting with your own emotions and memories takes a lot of courage. Being willing to turn your focus inward and explore your innermost thoughts and feelings is one of the hardest things that God asks us to do. "Wait," you might say. "When did God say that?"

Fair question. First John 2:6 tells us that "whoever abides in [Jesus] ought to walk in the same way in which he walked." Jesus is our standard. Jesus is the model of righteousness and right living.

But how can we know if we are following in Jesus' footsteps if we don't examine our own nature, our choices and behaviors, and our beliefs?

Second Corinthians states, "Examine yourselves to see whether you are in the faith. Test yourselves. Or do you not realize this about yourselves, that Jesus Christ is in you?"

Looking deep inside ourselves can be a terrifying proposition. What will we discover? Even more frightening, what if we can't control what we discover? The practice of inward focus often feels like a grown-up version of hiding from the monster lurking under your bed. If you don't acknowledge your own fear and pain, maybe they will go away, too?

Unfortunately, no.

Internal Family Systems guides us in this process of self-examination and healing. This practice involves taking the time to settle in with your thoughts and emotions, and becoming comfortable and open to the parts of yourself that you may typically try to avoid or reject.

As a therapist, I have found Internal Family Systems to be the most amazing, most comprehensive, most relatable therapy approach I've ever used in over three decades of working in the mental health field. If you want to learn more about IFS, I've created a resource section that can point you to more information. That said, I want to make sure to cover at least the basics for those who might be picking this up without ever having heard of IFS.

So, here we go:

Human beings are designed to avoid pain and to desire pleasure. This is why we learn to be careful around sharp, pointy things and salivate at the sight of juicy ripe berries. This is also why we try very hard to avoid feeling sad or distressed and why we so easily get ensnared by feel-good activities.

Unfortunately, our brain has also been designed by the Creator to take note of and remember experiences of pain, fear, and intense feelings because those states of being mean that something really big and important to our survival happened. What ends up happening is that we get stuck in a cycle of trying to avoid the painful memories and emotions that our brain is programmed to keep fresh and instantly accessible whenever needed.

To deal with this essential conflict (as well as the multitude of other complexities our brain has to juggle,) we have parts or subpersonalities that take on tasks and roles. These parts of ourselves hold their own beliefs, emotions, thoughts, and learned behaviors that help us function in both the inner world of our psyche and the outer world.

We use the concept of parts in our everyday language all the time without realizing it. "Part of me wants to go to the party but another part just wants to get into my jammies and curl up on the couch."

Another instance where we can see parts at work is when we're standing in front of the kitchen cupboard, staring at a package of Oreos. Double-stuffed. Lots of parts can get activated! A Craving part may be at odds with a Healthy Eating part, an Inner Critic may start to scold, or a Guilty/Shaming part may surface after the fact.

One more example...

Have you ever left an argument deeply regretting the things you said or did? Ever sit in confusion, wondering what came over you? You know that, deep down, you didn't mean those things you said. But in your anger, at that moment, a part of you might have. A part that was lashing out; a part that was protecting another part—a part that is in pain from earlier trauma or wounding. The conflict got too close to that wounded part and the lashing out part jumped in.

All of these parts are operating under the avoid-pain/find-pleasure principles, mentioned above. Parts are designed to interact with the world and with each other in ways that protect and benefit the whole person. Parts have their own systems for achieving these goals. Having parts is normal but when we live through trauma or relationship wounds these parts take on the burden of the emotional lived experience and they carry those burdens for us.

There are three categories of burdened parts—exiles, managers, and firefighters—that perform different functions and make up the systems of our inner world. Each part has their own job to do based on the experiences they have lived through, and they have each learned unique ways of coping with the ways they were wounded.

Exiles are the wounded parts of us. They carry the burden of the pain we encountered during traumatic events or through relationship wounding. The exile's job is to express and embody the deep wrong that was committed. They hold the injustice, the betrayal of trust, the loss of innocence, and the raw emotions of those experiences. People or circumstances made the exile believe that they are not good enough, are unlovable, are unworthy, are broken or damaged, or are helpless and eternally vulnerable. The exile took those "facts" to heart. This kind of pain was (and continues to be) too overwhelming to be endured so other parts—managers and firefighters—stepped forward to take on the mission of pain containment.

Managers dedicate themselves to protecting the exiles in a two-pronged approach. Internally, managers contain the exiles, stuffing the emotions down and cutting the exile off from expression. Externally, managers strive to create or control the environment, people, and circumstances in order to preemptively avoid situations that will ignite the exile's pain.

Managers also strive through their efforts and actions to disprove the exile's underlying beliefs of unworthiness or unlovability. If making mistakes exposed an exile to criticism and humiliation, a Perfectionist manager will obsess on each and every detail of a task to keep that from ever happening again. If living in chaos taught an exile to fear the unknown, a Worrier will stay up all night exploring and examining all the options of "what might happen next" to keep the unknown at bay.

Firefighters, on the other hand, are reactive. Firefighters leap into action when managers' efforts have somehow failed to keep the dams from overflowing and the exile from flooding the body with pain. The firefighter's only job is to numb or distract—by any means necessary. The firefighter doesn't care if you're on a diet or that you vowed not to drink on Tuesdays or that cutting your thigh only provides a momentary endorphin rush. The consequences—guilt, shame, relentless self-loathing—are not under the firefighters' jurisdiction. Their only duty is to numb or distract from the pain. Firefighters' behaviors are extreme because they have to be. Examples of firefighter coping skills include substance abuse/addictions, disordered eating, raging, self-harm, suicidality, and whatever other creative means of avoiding pain that our firefighters can come up with at the time.

When we look at our parts based solely on their behaviors, it can be hard to understand a central concept of Internal Family Systems, which is "All parts are welcome." How do you love all of yourself when so many of these parts are annoying or troublesome or even dangerous and scary?

Maybe another way to ask that question is "where am I in all of this chaos? Where is the core me?" IFS calls this core you, the Self. When Richard Schwartz was learning about this internal world from his clients, he noticed that there were times when they would speak about a part that was not a part. They described it as an aspect of themselves that was central to their identity. Self is an immutable pure essence of spirit that connects us to the wisdom inside and the wisdom of the Divine. As Christians, we are used to calling this aspect of ourselves our soul. My personal belief is that this essence is the animating breath of life that is breathed into each of us by the Creator. I also believe that Self is the intersection that opens space for the Holy Spirit to dwell within us.

This is where the healing begins.

LEARNING ABOUT YOUR PARTS

The following is a summarized version of Dr. Richard Schwartz's 6 F's technique for connecting with parts from Self.

Sit in a quiet place where you are unlikely to be interrupted. Turn off your phone or silence notifications on your devices. Take a couple of deep breaths and close your eyes. Allow your body to settle into itself. Feel your back against the chair or your sit bones pressing against the cushion. Press your feet against the floor, grounding yourself to the earth. Take another deep breath. When you are ready:

1) Invite the Holy Spirit to move in your heart as you take this quiet time with yourself and your parts.

2) Invite parts that may have come to your notice during the reading to connect with you.

Find the part(s) in or around your body. Open your heart and welcome them. If you feel resistance from other parts, you will need to get their permission before moving forward with getting to know the target part better.

Focus on the physical sensations and emotions that arise in your body when you notice the part. Parts use the body to communicate. Where, in or around your body, does this part express its protests or resistance? Check for tension, discomfort, pain, body sensations, focused energy, etc.

Flesh out your understanding of this part. Do you have an internal image of this part? Does it remind you of a character or a person that you know? Or do you sense it in your thoughts or as a "little voice" inside? Maybe it shows up as a shape or an energy? How old is it? What shall you call it? Take your time. Be curious.

After getting a deeper sense of the part's presence, ask yourself: How do I **feel** toward this part? Check to see if you are in Self by looking for the following characteristics: compassion, curiosity, confidence, courage, connection, clarity, calm, and creativity.

Become **friends** with the part. Get to know it better. Find out its back story. How does it believe it is helping? What is its job or mission? How did it learn that it was important to protect you in this way?

What does the part **fear** will happen if it doesn't do its job? How will you get hurt if it is not there to protect you? What does it need to feel safe enough to trust Self's leadership?

I HAVE PARTS?

FOR THE SPIRIT GOD GAVE US DOES NOT MAKE US TIMID, BUT GIVES US POWER, LOVE, AND SELF-DISCIPLINE. 2 TIMOTHY 1:7

We all have parts. Having parts is normal. It's human. Having parts is not proof of mental illness. Often when I'm first explaining IFS, I will have people asking if having parts is a sign that they're crazy. We have been socialized to view our thoughts, emotions, and physical bodies as being distinctly separate from each other. In particular, we believe that our thoughts can (and should) rule over our emotions and bodies.

But is that possible? Can you think away your emotions? I bet you've tried. I know I have, and it doesn't work. So, we think (there it is again) that we must be doing it wrong, so we try to logic our emotions into submission. "There is no reason for me to not trust my spouse. Yes, I've been hurt deeply before but not by him. I know I should just trust him but it's so hard." Or how about this: "I know I don't really need that donut so why can't I stop thinking about eating it? There must be something wrong with me. I'm disgusting." Or this: "I know I'm good enough for that promotion but what if I'm not? Worse, what if I go for it and then they find out how little I really do know? What if they discover that I'm just a fraud?"

All people have parts. All people have, to some degree or other, *burdened* parts. Trauma, which in this sense includes abuse or neglect, places these burdens on our parts. Parts have to navigate this world and when the world is scary and dangerous these parts assume jobs to deal with the disordered world they are stuck in. Children are born into dysfunction. They have to cope as best they can in a dangerous and unpredictable world with only the limited number of tools they can scrape together. Trauma teaches these parts certain "life lessons:"

I'm not important enough to be taken care of.

Mistakes are humiliating.

If I make others happy, they won't rage.

It's my job to take care of my mom/dad/siblings because somebody has to.

Wounds are created. Beliefs about our worth, our identity, relationships, and the world are formed and set in concrete in our brain because these lessons literally made a difference in our ability to survive. Behaviors and patterns of reaction become seemingly automatic. Emotions are walled off or buried.

Sometimes the scope of this journey of healing and reconciling the past can feel daunting. But we are not alone in this venture. Second Timothy tells us that God gave us a spirit without fear, a spirit of power and love and self-control. Healing comes from the Holy Spirit. Giving love and grace to those wounded parts (even the annoying ones!) that have taken the blows from a fallen world is a kindness that you can finally extend to yourself.

Thoughts to ponder: How do you feel, deep down, about the concept of parts and Self? Are you ready to commit to new lessons? Ones that teach you how to love yourself?

ALL PARTS ARE WELCOME

"I TELL YOU, LOVE YOUR ENEMIES. HELP AND GIVE WITHOUT EXPECTING A RETURN. YOU'LL NEVER - I PROMISE - REGRET IT. LIVE OUT THIS GOD-CREATED IDENTITY THE WAY OUR FATHER LIVES TOWARD US, GENEROUSLY AND GRACIOUSLY, EVEN WHEN WE'RE AT OUR WORST. LUKE 6: 32-42

One of the most important declarations that IFS makes is: All parts are welcome. In our day-to-day life, most find that it's not too difficult to appreciate managers, those over-worked, always striving parts that keep us functioning in the day to day. It's easy to feel good about the parts that at least try to help us succeed in life. In fact, a lot of us want to be our managers. Getting rid of those troublesome firefighters and pain-filled exiles would, we imagine, solve an awful lot of problems. Firefighters, in particular, are the parts that bring us to our knees. We can't control them and the harder we try, the wilder and more out of control they get. The after-effects of their choices trigger Shame and/or our Inner Critic, both of whom get busy scolding the firefighter to "never do that again!!" And what about our lost, little exiles with their awful burdens of anguish? We bury them and then enlist managers and firefighters to keep them contained, thus protecting us from feeling their pain.

Stuff down the exiles; chase after the elusive perfection that the managers promise; get rid of the firefighters…

It's exhausting. And it doesn't work.

So where does that leave us? Saying "All parts are welcome" means opening our Self to understanding and accepting these troublesome, embarrassing, or vilified parts of ourselves. It's a lot like the grace Jesus extends to all sinners. He chose his friends and followers from the most despised groups of society. He physically touched lepers. He defended adulterers. He took notice of and delighted in vulnerable children. In fact, for the religious leaders of that time, one of the most maddening things about Jesus *was* his acceptance of these "unclean," rejected souls. Jesus was well aware that it is hard to love troublemakers and unpleasant persons. Thinking about our parts as enemies or as things to be rid of only makes matters worse.

Love the unlovable. Love the unloved.

Thoughts to ponder: What part of yourself have you wanted to simply get rid of? What if, instead of pushing it away, you try to get to know it better?

THREE-IN-ONE

Jesus answered: "Don't you know me, Philip, even after I have been among you such a long time? Anyone who has seen me has seen the Father. How can you say, 'Show us the Father'? Don't you believe that I am in the Father and that the Father is in me? The words I say to you I do not speak on my own authority. Rather, it is the Father, living in me, who is doing his work. Believe me when I say that I am in the Father and the Father is in me, or at least believe on the evidence of the works themselves. Very truly I tell you, whoever believes in me will do the works I have been doing, and they will do even greater things than these because I am going to the Father. And I will do whatever you ask in my name, so that the Father may be glorified in the Son. You may ask me for anything in my name, and I will do it. If you love

ME, KEEP MY COMMANDS. AND I WILL ASK THE FATHER, AND HE WILL GIVE YOU ANOTHER ADVOCATE TO HELP YOU AND BE WITH YOU FOREVER--THE SPIRIT OF TRUTH. THE WORLD CANNOT ACCEPT HIM, BECAUSE IT NEITHER SEES HIM NOR KNOWS HIM. BUT YOU KNOW HIM, FOR HE LIVES WITH YOU AND WILL BE IN YOU. JOHN 14:9-17

When I was first learning about Internal Family Systems the biggest stumbling block was the idea of multiplicity--having subpersonalities. It's a difficult concept and one I wanted to make sure was consistent with Biblical truth and God's design. Western society focuses so much on the intellect--our thinking brain--as being the whole of our personality. Most of us believe that how and what we think defines who we are. Emotions and physical sensations in our body are pushed aside as not as important as what our logical brain tells us. Worse, emotions and our bodies are seen as treacherous liars that interfere with the "higher purpose" of our brains. That perspective has contributed to the belief that we are single-minded entities ruled by our logic and the quality of our thoughts.

But is that how God designed us? The Bible tells us we are made in God's image. It also tells us that God exists as three distinct persons, yet He is one being. Each person of the Trinity has a unique, separate, distinct identity yet still incorporates the wholeness of One. They are parts of the whole if you will.

Colossians 1:15-17 tells us that Christ, the Son, is the visible image of the invisible God. Christ was not created by God because Jesus is "the one through whom God created everything in heaven and earth."

The same is true for the Holy Spirit. The Spirit was also present at creation. (Genesis 1:2) A few verses later we see that God refers to Himself in plural form in the original Hebraic text. In doing so He is revealing Himself as a plurality in unity—Three-in-One—all in existence and present for the creation.

The Trinity is also revealed at Jesus' baptism where, once again, all three Persons of God are present and all three are doing something different. Jesus is being baptized, the Holy Spirit is seen "descending on [Jesus] like a dove," and God's voice from above is speaking of his pleasure in his son.

Thoughts to ponder: What does the apparent multiplicity of God tell us about ourselves? How do you feel about conceptualizing yourself as having multiple parts and a centered Self?

Namaste, Parts

RATHER, IT SHOULD BE THAT YOUR INNER SELF, THE UNFADING BEAUTY OF A GENTLE AND QUIET SPIRIT, WHICH IS OF GREAT WORTH IN GOD'S SIGHT. 1 PETER 3:4

How do relationships fare if we don't put time and effort into them? Usually not very well. The same is true in our relationship between Self and parts. Getting to know our parts, hearing their stories, and fostering the healing process is truly remarkable but it's just the beginning of a lifelong journey of Self-knowledge and Self-love.

It's okay to love yourself. In fact, it's *essential* to love yourself. God does. Why shouldn't you?

So, how *do* we nurture a loving relationship with our Self? The quick answer is through time and effort.

Take time every day. Find a quiet place, if you can. Take some deep, slow breaths. Turn your attention inward and invite your parts to come and sit with you. Be patient. Be curious. Be open. Listen.

Be still.

Take your time. Introductions can feel awkward. We aren't always sure if we are going to like the other person or them, us. Before we can decide, we have to find out more about the other. We look for similarities and shared experiences. We look for potential conflicts or differences of opinion. We look for interesting characteristics. And there are always surprises.

It's the same process when we are getting to know ourselves. Once we are introduced to the idea that we have parts of ourselves, then building a relationship becomes a matter of learning about this inner world, increasing communication between Self and parts and part-to-part as well, and above all, building trust. Learning to trust your Self means learning to love all of you, from the inside, out. Everything we would do if we were cultivating a relationship with a new potential friend or romantic interest, we do with our parts as well.

Be available. Be intentional. Commit to spending time together. Be attentive. Be compassionate about stories or memories that are shared. Trust their sincerity. Respect boundaries. Comfort sadness. Be tender about fears.

Thoughts to ponder: What action steps are you taking to get to know your parts? Are you ready to commit to showing up, being present, and being curious about your parts?

IN THE BEGINNING

"THERE IS NO FEAR IN LOVE, BUT PERFECT LOVE CASTS OUT FEAR. FOR FEAR HAS TO DO WITH PUNISHMENT, AND WHOEVER FEARS HAS NOT BEEN PERFECTED IN LOVE. WE LOVE BECAUSE HE FIRST LOVED US." 1 JOHN 4:18-19

Why do we have to keep remembering things we truly don't want to remember? If that was then and this is now, why do we have to keep remembering? Can't we just move on? Forget about it? Set our sight on the future and let go of the past?

Unfortunately, no. Besides, you've probably tried that already.

Maybe it would help to understand a little bit about how the brain works and why.

The Creator designed the human brain to first create a memory of the horrible thing that happened. A memory *preserves*, in minute detail, the lived experience of the pain that we felt when the bad thing was happening. We don't like to remember those thoughts, emotions, or feelings. Feeling those things again is really difficult. But our brain (designed by God, remember?) knows that we have to remember the important information about how we survived that bad thing because we might end up in a similar situation in the future. Information that the fear or sadness born in that moment of grief or terror told your brain was important to your survival (physically, emotionally, psychologically, or spiritually). When something triggers that memory the brain kicks into survival mode, flooding us with the emotions, fears, and reactions that were created during the trauma so that we can use what we learned to get out of the situation again. The brain recognizes that remembering is critical to our survival.

That's not all. Even though remembering these awful things is excruciatingly painful, the Creator also designed our brain to *prioritize* access to that awful memory. That means the brain will have instantaneous access to that memory whenever we are confronted with similar situations. Sometimes this can feel completely random. We don't always understand why a trauma reaction is triggered, which can be frustrating. Scary, even. The thing is the brain can't waste time sorting out what is a real threat or what isn't. It's too dangerous to pause or reflect on what might be happening and whether it is a real danger or not. The brain reacts instantly, then sorts it out later. This keeps us safe.

Memories aren't the only thing created in moments of trauma and wounding. Parts get assigned certain tasks and missions. A soon-to-be-exiled part picks up the burden of the lesson that was learned when the bad thing happened, and they carry it for us. When a new danger triggers us, the brain kicks in with an emergency response reaction and the exile relives the pain or terror of the original event. That becomes excruciatingly difficult, so we develop parts to deal with the exiles, and managers and firefighters become burdened with their mission to protect the exiles too.

A system of protection is created. This system will continue to operate in this emergency-readiness mode until these parts feel loved and safe again.

The good news: Love—genuine love for ourselves, for each other, and for God—will overcome all fear.

Thoughts to ponder: Have you ever gotten frustrated with the way the past keeps cropping up when all you want to do is forget it? What do you think about God's design for survival: preserving critical information in the form of a memory and activating that memory in an instant whenever it may be needed?

STUCK

THERE IS NO FEAR IN LOVE, BUT PERFECT LOVE CASTS OUT FEAR. FOR FEAR HAS TO DO WITH PUNISHMENT, AND WHOEVER FEARS HAS NOT BEEN PERFECTED IN LOVE. 1 JOHN 4:18

When parts become burdened at a young age, they tend to get stuck there. Stuck in the past, stuck at the age they were when they were somehow assigned the job of coping with an impossible task.

Children—by definition—are immature. They lack experience, have extremely limited coping skills, are often impulsive, and have poor control over their emotions. Is it any wonder that parts created out of childhood traumas fall apart when triggered? They are little children with very grown-up problems.

Worse, the solutions they came up with years ago no longer work. An Avoiding Conflict part which used to calm an irate parent now creates problems with poor communication skills at work. Being a Rule Follower used to please our teachers, but now it's called controlling by our spouse and kids. Drinking used to calm our parts, now it gives us a hangover and it makes us feel guilty and ashamed of our lack of control. Being a So Careful part used to help us avoid mistakes, and therefore embarrassment, but now we are called picky and perfectionistic.

What once worked, now feels broken.

A part of us knows we're screwing up. Other parts are brought on board and tasked with fixing the formerly useful parts. Guilt and the Inner Critic set up a constant barrage of scolding and harsh criticism designed to bully now-ineffective parts into not doing the thing these parts were trained to do. Guilt says to Rule Follower: "Why can't you just lighten up? Can't you see you're ruining the whole day?" Critic says to Drinker: "You are disgusting! Do you even remember what you did last night?"

Patterns of self-loathing are set up and no matter how hard we try, we just keep doing what we don't want to do and hating ourselves for it.

Hate doesn't heal. Love does. Love is the only power that can lift us up and set us on a new course. That means learning to love ourselves. Learning to let God love us. Learning to let others love us, too.

Thoughts to ponder: Do you feel stuck? What patterns have your parts fallen into as they try to navigate the present with the strategies they used to use in the past?

THE GREAT FLOOD

But I pray to you, Lord, in the time of your favor, in your great love, O God, answer me with your sure salvation. Rescue me from the mire, do not let me sink; deliver me from those who hate me, from the deep waters. Do not let the floodwaters engulf me or the depths swallow me up or the pit close its mouth over me. Answer me, Lord, out of the goodness of your love; in your great mercy turned to me. Do not hide your face from your servant; answer me quickly, for I am in trouble. Come near and rescue me; deliver me because of my foes.   Psalm 69:13-18

Floods are scary. They are destructive, chaotic forces of nature—a pretty apt description of what it feels like when we become flooded with painful emotions. The fear of being swept away is very real. Fear of drowning in the raw expanse of pain is the primary reason that exiles get exiled in the first place.

If this fear isn't adequately addressed and permission from protective parts granted, then healing can't happen. The protectors need to trust you enough—not completely, but just enough—to grant permission to work with an exile. Trust is formed by building a relationship, and that takes time.

Noah took seventy years to build the ark and he used God's design to do so. God wasn't in a hurry. He didn't ask Noah to sling a couple boards together and build a simple raft to face the Flood. Good things take time.

So, take time to build your relationships with this inner world. Let your Spirit-led Self commune with the Holy Spirit and let him lead the way. Make a commitment to open your heart to the workings of these protective and hurting parts.

Thoughts to ponder: Are you ready and willing to do what it takes to build relationships with your inner world parts?

SO TIRED

THE APOSTLES GATHERED AROUND JESUS AND REPORTED TO HIM ALL THEY HAD DONE AND TAUGHT. THEN, BECAUSE SO MANY PEOPLE WERE COMING AND GOING THAT THEY DID NOT EVEN HAVE A CHANCE TO EAT, HE SAID TO THEM, "COME WITH ME BY YOURSELVES TO A QUIET PLACE AND GET SOME REST." MARK 6:30-31

A manager part's job is to function, to keep the whole she-bang moving forward, one way or another. And, more importantly, to keep you so busy with "good, productive work" that there is no time for an exile to emerge or even be noticed.

Because that is the primary duty of all managers: Keep the exile in its cage. Nice and quiet. In the dark. Contained. DON'T POKE IT!

But it's so exhausting. It takes so much energy to keep the mask on, the train rolling, the production line moving, the To-Do list growing. Don't slow down. Don't look back. And for goodness' sake, don't stop!

No rest for the weary. Because resting means stopping and stopping means the exile might awaken. Perhaps that is why self-care seems so unattainable with all of its "relax," "get in touch with your emotions," and "listen to your body signals."

Managers are desperate to create a reality that is the polar opposite of the exiles' beliefs. Do you have an exile that believes you are a failure? Then you either have managers that push and drive you toward success or you have managers that avoid challenges in order to prevent proving the exile is correct. Or you have both!

Jesus offers rest and sustenance. He has been with people who were so hurried that they couldn't slow down, even for him. When he saw how hard they were pushing themselves, he gently reminded them of the importance of quiet and the peace that only exists when we abide in his presence.

Thoughts to ponder: Jesus is inviting you to come to him. Just you. Just as you are. Meet with him in a quiet place and rest. Check inside and see how different parts are responding to Jesus' invitation to rest and be with him.

PAINPRINTS

A MAN WITH LEPROSY CAME AND KNELT BEFORE JESUS AND SAID, "LORD, IF YOU ARE WILLING, YOU CAN MAKE ME CLEAN." JESUS REACHED OUT HIS HAND AND TOUCHED THE MAN. "I AM WILLING," HE SAID. "BE CLEAN!" IMMEDIATELY THE MAN WAS CLEANSED OF HIS LEPROSY. MATT 8: 2-3

Exiles hold the pain. The particular pain each carries is as unique to us as our fingerprints. I guess you could think of them as "painprints." Pain comes in many flavors: sadness, loneliness, rejection, abandonment... Who likes to feel those? Nobody, right? So, most of us get very good at stuffing those feelings down, shoving them away, and silencing them. The exiles of our inner world: the lepers, the unclean, the untouchables. We trap our managers and firefighters into a never-ending cycle of protecting and silencing our exiles, and we engage in a fruitless struggle to "leave the past in the past." Does that work for you? Because it has never worked for me.

Jesus had a unique approach to the Untouchables. He touched them. And those who had been silenced? He listened. And he loved. Oh, how he loved! He waded right into their messy, unclean lives and loved all over the outcasts. Jesus shows us how to heal the exiles' pain. They long to be seen. They long to be heard. Above all, they crave redemption. And through that process of being seen and heard, through compassionate intercession, our exiles will be healed.

Thoughts to ponder: Are you willing to love your exiles? What part(s) might be resisting those efforts?

POLAR OPPOSITES

Therefore if you have any encouragement from being united with Christ, if any comfort from his love, if any common sharing in the Spirit, if any tenderness and compassion, then make my joy complete by being like-minded, having the same love, being one in spirit and of one mind. Do nothing out of selfish ambition or vain conceit. Rather, in humility value others above yourself, not looking to your own interests but each of you to the interests of the others. In your relationships with one another, have the same mindset as Christ Jesus. Phil 2:1-5

Have you ever made a decision to go with Plan A and not five minutes later are equally convinced that Plan B is the only way to go? It's easy to identify parts in those situations. Parts at war with each other. One part wants to go in one direction while another wants to go a completely different way. Without understanding your inner world, it can feel like you're going crazy! And there is probably yet another part who's telling you to "just make a decision already" or may even be calling you names, trying to shame you into action. "Any action! Just choose!"

Parts have different experiences, different goals, and different imperatives. Your People-Pleaser whose mission is to sustain relationships by making others happy may be in direct conflict with an Ambitious part whose job it is to make sure you are moving ahead in your career and who wants you to throw your hat into the ring for a new promotion. A Perfectionist may be so rigid in meeting its own high (impossible) standards that an exhausted Procrastinator steps in to slow things down. A part that wants to be healthy or lose weight may run up against a part that finds comfort from TV binging, sugars, fats, and carbs.

Managers and firefighters are almost always in conflict. Managers keep trying to steer the boat into smoother waters and firefighters are content with blowing it up. It doesn't seem like there's a lot of common ground there.

But there is. Both managers and firefighters share the same goal: pain management. They just go at the job in vastly different ways. Managers are preemptive. They strive to prevent pain from surfacing in the first place.

Firefighters are reactive. They leap into action when the pain threatens to escape or overwhelm them. Firefighters focus on saving the moment--no matter the consequences.

Once we learn to communicate and build relationships between Self and parts, our parts can work on healing. Negotiations can take place or a truce can be declared. Cooperation and compromises can be explored. We become unified and our inner world, more harmonious.

Thoughts to ponder: Do you sometimes feel at war with yourself? How might parts be united with each other and united with Christ help that inner turmoil?

BIG JOBS

WHEN JESUS SAW THIS, HE WAS INDIGNANT. HE SAID TO THEM, "LET THE LITTLE CHILDREN COME TO ME, AND DO NOT HINDER THEM, FOR THE KINGDOM OF GOD BELONGS TO SUCH AS THESE. MARK 10:14

Most burden parts are formed in childhood and, as such, are really like children playing dress-up in their adult roles. They are stuck in the past believing they are fighting the same monsters that they faced back then. This is especially true for exiles who are prisoners in their pain, their very existence a threat to the parts that protect them. Burdened parts learned one way to protect these exiles and it is their mission in life to keep handling those triggers in the same way—even if it doesn't work anymore. It's like they were given a hammer when they were five years old and told to keep hitting the nail. So, they approach every subsequent problem by hitting it with a hammer, even if hammer-hitting is now causing massive problems in their life. They don't understand it. *Why isn't the hammer working? Why are people and other parts angry at the hammering? Doesn't anyone see that hammering is the only thing that makes sense and keeps us safe?*

It's easy to get frustrated with these hammer-wielding child parts because they frequently create a big mess out of things. But if we can create a space inside, a space where we can gently ask these parts how they are helping, we can take a step away from frustration and open ourselves up to feeling compassion or even appreciation for these valiant little soldiers.

Thoughts to ponder: How do you feel toward these parts? As annoying as they might be, can you understand the reasons why they began acting as they do?

IGNORE THEM AT YOUR PERIL

For the moment all discipline seems painful rather than pleasant, but later it yields the peaceable fruit of righteousness to those who have been trained by it. Therefore, lift your drooping hands and gather your weak knees, and make straight paths for your feet, so that what is lame may not be put out of joint but rather be healed. Heb 12:11-13

Make no mistake—doing the relationship building involved in getting to know your parts is not easy. At the start, most of us feel overwhelmed and maybe even discouraged about the scope of the journey. That's normal, but don't let it stop you. Because the truth of the matter is, we're going to have to deal or live with the reactions of our parts one way or another. Unfortunately, our attempts to stuff parts down or shove them away also come with a price.

One of the most common ways that parts express themselves is through the experience of blending. Blending simply means a part is expressing itself so intensely that it feels as if you are fully that part. Some people describe it as if they were "set on autopilot." Later, there is often an instinctive recognition that you weren't behaving like the "real" you. Things are said that, deep down, we don't really mean but in the moment of blending, parts are lashing out, hurting as they have been hurt.

If you are unaware of or not in a relationship with parts, you have no influence on them or their behavior. It is only through a trusting relationship with Self that parts can learn new ways of dealing with old problems. Without this trusting relationship, parts just keep doing what parts do because that's all they know how to do.

One other method that parts use to express themselves is through the body. Parts can be a literal pain in the neck (or head, back, stomach, GI, etc.). Like a child begging for attention, our parts will use any means necessary to get what they believe they need. If we avoid doing the work of building and nurturing relationships with ourselves, we will be sorry.

Thoughts to ponder: How do your parts make themselves known when you won't listen to them?

THE BEST ME

FOR THE SPIRIT GOD GAVE US DOES NOT MAKE US TIMID, BUT GIVES US POWER, LOVE, AND SELF-DISCIPLINE. 2 TIMOTHY 1:7

I have to confess, there is a part of me that wants to grow up to be my managers. (Yes, that means I have a manager part that idolizes my other manager parts.) My managers seem to have the right idea as far as being organized, getting things done, and doing the right things. They're always busy. They are future-focused and ambitious. For the most part, they seem to be trying to present me as the "best me that I can be." That's not a bad thing.

We must also remember that not all of our parts have been burdened with unhealthy or trauma-born weights. Everybody has parts that work for our best interests and managers are a big aspect of that. For instance, I have a Learner part. I love learning. Learning is good. The only time problems develop is if my Learner takes over and doesn't allow other parts to function as they need to function. If I use learning as a method to distract from anything painful that might be going on in my life or use it as a way to intellectualize something I should be letting myself feel, then learning can be a way of avoiding an emotion rather than abiding with it.

Burdened managers are convinced that they know the best and therefore only way of behaving and reacting. Sometimes that kind of certainty gives us an alluring—but often false—sense of security. We call these parts "self-like" managers.

Two ways to distinguish between a self-like manager and your Self are to look for mercy and to check for an agenda. If you fall short of the manager's expectations, how does it make you feel? Do you then struggle with disappointment? Shame? Panic? Those are not aspects of Self. Self is about being, not doing. Because Self doesn't have an agenda, it doesn't have fear attached to the outcome. Sounds a lot like faith, doesn't it? Gentle compassion, recognition of an honest effort, curiosity about what might happen next—those are Self. Take care not to confuse the rigid certainty of a manager with the rich confidence of Self.

Thoughts to ponder: What aspects of your managers do you find easy to admire?

Unlikely Heroes

For God so loved the world that he gave his one and only Son, that whoever believes in him shall not perish but have eternal life. For God did not send his Son into the world to condemn the world, but to save the world through him. John 3:16-17

Pretty much everyone would agree that those brave men and women whose job it is to run into burning buildings while the rest of us are running away are heroes, plain and simple. *Firefighters*. (May God bless them all and keep them safe from harm.)

In IFS, we have a type of protector that is called firefighters because they also rush in when the internal flames are raging, when all seems to be exploding in our internal world. Unfortunately, it is often difficult to see these parts as heroes. In fact, firefighters are rather easy to hate. At least, before you get to know them and understand who they are protecting and why.

That's because in their headlong rush to help when an exile's pain seems to be overwhelming the system, internal firefighters will often choose behaviors that cause as many problems as they seek to resolve. Drinking, over-eating, gambling, raging, pushing people we love away, even suicidal wishes, etc. All of these behaviors are designed to distract or numb.

They mean well. They really do. Firefighters try to counteract the exile's intense, overflowing emotions by reaching for the first "feel good" substance or activity that they can grasp. They aren't trying to mess things up. They are trying to help in the only way that they know how. They throw themselves into the breach of the exile's overwhelming pain, sacrificing themselves to bring the system back to baseline.

Jesus was an unlikely hero. Aside from his lineage, there was nothing about his circumstances that would have screamed "Messiah." Many Jews of that time were expecting the messiah to show up as a royal military leader who would overthrow their enemies. Instead, they got a baby born in a shabby out-building and a leader executed like a criminal, his body laid to rest in a borrowed tomb.

We got the Prince of Peace. He came to take away our pain and suffering, sacrificing himself for our sins. For all their faults, firefighters try to do the same thing: to take away our pain. They also sacrifice themselves. We may not like the consequences—and that's okay—but we can at least acknowledge the heart of the firefighter.

Thoughts to ponder: How do you feel toward your firefighters? The drinker, the drug user, the over-eater, the spender, the rage monster, and yes, even the part who offers death as a "final solution" to the question, "How long can I stand to be in this unbearable pain?" Can you see what they are trying to protect you from?

DO YOU SEE WHAT I SEE?

LONG AGO AT MANY TIMES AND IN MANY
WAYS, GOD SPOKE TO OUR FATHERS BY THE
PROPHETS, BUT IN THESE LAST DAYS HE
HAS SPOKEN TO US BY HIS SON, WHOM
HE APPOINTED THE HEIR OF ALL THINGS,
THROUGH WHOM HE ALSO CREATED THE
WORLD. HEB 1: 1-2

I don't know if anyone has ever taken a survey but being able to visually imagine parts is pretty common. Often the image is of a younger version of that person, perhaps wearing a favorite outfit or a "snapshot" of the child self captured in a particular memory like hiding behind the couch. Sometimes the image is more of a caricature like an old witch or an uptight little accountant with thick glasses and a clipboard.

I don't usually see images of people. And I was reassured to learn that Richard Swartz, founder of Internal Family Systems, doesn't see his inner parts, either.

Fact is, parts show up in a variety of different ways: images, thoughts (cognitions), voices, physical sensations, and even specific movements or postures. For me, my parts typically communicate by thoughts and physical tensions or pains. When my Family-Harmony part gets activated by an argument between family members, I'll feel a deep, heavy weight in my chest and a thick, rising sense of despair. My thoughts fluctuate between "I have to fix this" to "Make them stop!"

It's different when I meditate, though. When I am intentional about making contact with my inner world, I see balls of energy, different colors, and different shapes. "Fear of Future" is a wildly anxious, amorphous ball of yellow green (bile, if you will) jittery, spikey, vibrating energy. It darts around a lot. Kinda skittish. Its questions are "What are we going to do?" and "How can I fix this?" It's allied with a lumpy, dark gray, slush-mud energy called "Dread." Dread makes my shoulders cramp into knots of tension and gives me headaches.

Similarly, how God shows up for each of us is just as varied. For some, He's an actual voice, maybe a whisper. For others, the Holy Spirit moves within, giving gentle (or not so gentle) nudges to guide our direction. God speaks through the Word, through music, through nature, through other people and so many more ways.

The way God or your parts talk to you is not as important as being assured that they do communicate, one way or another. It is our duty to become familiar with the unique communication style that each uses to express themselves.

Thoughts to ponder: How do your parts communicate with you? How does God?

THE FIRST STEP

DRAW NEAR TO GOD AND HE WILL COME NEAR TO YOU. JAMES 4:8

Relationships take work. You can't expect to have a vital, ever-growing connection with someone that you routinely ignore. Keep that up long enough and the relationship withers and dies. The same thing happens with our internal relationships. Likewise, our relationship with God.

The first step in nurturing any relationship is to simply notice the other person's existence. See them. Acknowledge their importance in your life. Be present with them. Give them time and attention.

But sometimes... Sometimes the idea of "making friends" with beings we can't see or touch (God and/or our Parts) can feel... awkward. Weird. How do you start? What do you say? What if something goes wrong?

Like every relationship, we start by responding with curiosity to the parts we notice. Be open to learning about their unique personality and life experiences. Parts have different jobs, different ways of viewing the world, and different hopes and fears. Just like people. The way to learn about those differences is to ask. Believe it or not, parts will respond. They appreciate simply being noticed. Attention makes them feel loved and valued. Also, just like people!

It pleases God when we notice Him, too. The more intentional we are in slowing down and noticing God's presence in the moments of our day, the more clearly, we will be able to hear his gentle whisper or feel His presence in our life. Take time to notice God throughout the day. If you invite Him into the different areas of your life, He will show up for you.

Thoughts to ponder: How can you remind yourself to slow down and take notice of your parts throughout the day? How can you remind yourself to do the same for God?

SITTING ON THE ASH HEAP

IF I AM GUILTY—WOE TO ME! EVEN IF I AM INNOCENT, I CANNOT LIFT MY HEAD, FOR I AM FULL OF SHAME AND DROWNED IN MY AFFLICTION. JOB 10:15

Guilt and shame can be useful emotions and, under specific circumstances, are entirely appropriate to feel. Feeling guilty should occur when we recognize that we have done something wrong and regret having done that wrong thing. Shame arises in relationship with other people. We did a wrong thing and are aware that others judge our wrong actions accordingly. Stepping outside the approval of the community creates a pervasive feeling of unworthiness. Guilt is regret about something we have done, but shame involves how we feel about ourselves and what we believe others think of us. Both guilt and shame are supposed to correct future behavior and keep us in line with the moral code of our community. These emotions are negative motivators designed to keep us from repeating undesirable behavior. And that's not a bad thing, is it?

But sometimes a burdened part will experience guilt and shame in ways that are excessive and very unhealthy. Guilt and shame become a state of being rather than a pair of transitory emotions that dissipate once their jobs are done. Instead, some burdened parts use guilt and shame as a weapon, a constant, relentless scourge meant to punish us into perfection.

God did not design you to feel guilt and shame all the time.

Job's friends tried to make Job admit his guilt, even though Job didn't believe he had sinned. They assumed that all of the bad things that had befallen Job must have resulted from something Job had done wrong. Job had already gone through a long period of self-examination (ash heaps are good for that, apparently) and he held firm to his belief that he was not guilty of wrongdoing in the eyes of the Lord and didn't deserve to feel shame. It must have been difficult for Job to stand firm in the face of his friends' accusations.

Thoughts to ponder: Do you have a part(s) that uses guilt or shame as a way to shape your thoughts or behaviors? Sit for a few minutes with this part and find out a little more about it. Be curious. How are these guilt/shame parts trying to help?

TELL ME WHERE IT HURTS

AND AFTER YOU HAVE SUFFERED A LITTLE WHILE, THE GOD OF ALL GRACE, WHO HAS CALLED YOU TO HIS ETERNAL GLORY IN CHRIST, WILL HIMSELF RESTORE, CONFIRM, STRENGTHEN, AND ESTABLISH YOU. 1 PETER 5:10

Pain is a message, and that message should never be ignored. However, sometimes family belief systems teach us to "Stop whining!" "Be tough!" "Rub some dirt on it." They mean well. Those "be tough" messages are usually meant to encourage us to not give up. They are an attempt to create a spirit of toughness that will help us cope in a harsh world. Those messages feel strong and powerful. What's more, they often work! Telling ourselves to be tough pushes us to persevere during hardships and, hopefully, will lead to victory over them.

But those Be Tough beliefs also encourage us to ignore what may be very important information.

Physical pain is God's way of telling us to stop doing the thing that is causing pain. Continuing on may result in serious injury. Pain is our body's way of asking for a time out.

Emotional pain shows up in our bodies, too. Headaches, tension, gastrointestinal issues, exhaustion, back pain, exhaustion, muscular tension or tightness, etc. are all ways that our body speaks out on behalf of emotional or spiritual pain. While any of these might be traced back to physical or medical ailments, it's also very possible that a part or parts may be expressing themselves through the body. Parts really *can* be a pain in the neck.

Not only that, but parts that are ignored or rejected will double down on their efforts to communicate their protest so it's just not wise to ignore or pretend them away.

Sometimes God uses pain—emotional, physical, or spiritual—to get our attention, too. I don't necessarily believe that God causes the pain, but he certainly doesn't waste it! Pain is unpleasant; it's meant to be. Pain is designed to signal to us that there is a problem that needs to be faced. The quicker we acknowledge the pain the sooner we can get help for it.

Thoughts to ponder: In what ways do your parts use pain (physical, emotional, or spiritual) to get your attention? Do you listen to these signals or do you have parts that avoid, stuff down, or soldier through the pain?

IN THIS CORNER...

A FOOL TAKES NO PLEASURE IN UNDERSTANDING BUT ONLY IN EXPRESSING HIS OPINION. PROVERBS 18:2

Ironically, managers and firefighters share the same mission in life—protect the exiles, no matter what. So, you would think that sharing this heroic mission would give them something in common, right?

Nope. In fact, they despise one another.

Although managers and firefighters are tasked with protecting a common exile, they do *not* go at it in the same way. Firefighters swoop in to save the day, but they tend to leave a big mess behind for the managers to clean up. Managers are not amused. "Crazy, reckless, irresponsible!" groans the manager.

Firefighters don't care. After all, if managers were doing their jobs in the first place, firefighters wouldn't have to get involved. "Weak, whiny, rigid managers!" sneers the firefighter.

It's not pretty.

Firefighters and managers are unable to see the other's perspective. Not unlike our own relationships when we get so caught up in the "rightness" of our own point of view. Our society seems to have lost the ability to respect differing opinions. Accepting a different viewpoint is easier if we take the time to understand how and why the person or part came to that belief.

Once we are willing to seek an understanding of another's perspective, they become more open to doing the same. We still may not agree with each other, and that's okay. It's not necessary to agree in order to feel respect and compassion for another's experiences and perspective.

Thoughts to ponder: Do you have times when you find it difficult to appreciate someone's differing opinion? What comes up, inside, when a part of you is in opposition with another part? How does your body express the presence of inner conflict?

MEAN PARTS

LET NO CORRUPTING TALK COME OUT OF
YOUR MOUTHS, BUT ONLY SUCH AS IS
GOOD FOR BUILDING YOU UP, AS FITS THE
OCCASION, THAT IT MAY GIVE GRACE TO
THOSE WHO HEAR. EPH 4:29

Beating ourselves up, shaming, criticizing, nagging, rejecting, discounting, shunning, punishing, ignoring, loathing, numbing, minimizing, bullying, and/or reasoning away difficult emotions or memories doesn't work. That's a lot of things that don't work, yet our managers keep trying the same things, over and over again. Despite a resounding lack of success, these "Beat Yourself Up" parts cling to the notion that harsh criticism and shame are effective ways of dealing with pain. They try to shame the pain away.

Rejection doesn't heal. Love does.

James tells us the tongue is like a flame. It has great power, for both lifting and destroying. James calls the tongue "a restless evil, full of deadly poison." But there is good as well. That same tongue praises the Lord.

Words matter. Thoughts matter. Using shame as a tool to shape our behavior is outrageously ineffective. Time-consuming, too. Inner Critic parts often create loops of shame-filled thoughts and memories, sometimes going back decades to dredge up our failures—all in an attempt to keep us on track.

Ironically, one of the most common ways that we react to an Inner Critic is to... well... shame it. "I hate the part of me that is so negative! I wish it would just stop!" Negativity begets negativity. But happily, love and encouragement work the same way.

Love and encouragement toward the Inner Critic, that is. Yikes! Here we are trying to get the Inner Critic to be nicer to us, but it really works the other way around. Without a loving relationship with our Self, our parts won't heal.

Thoughts to ponder: Do you have a part that uses shame to beat you up? How is it trying to help? What is it trying to accomplish? Do you have another part that hates the shaming part?

LAUGH 'TIL IT HURTS

A JOYFUL HEART IS GOOD MEDICINE, BUT
A CRUSHED SPIRIT DRIES UP THE BONES.
PROVERBS 17:22

I like to make people laugh. It's a really cool thing to see someone crack up at something I said. Humor often brings people together. I'm pretty sure Jesus could tell a good joke, and God definitely has a sense of humor.

But, like all things, humor has a dark side such as when we use humor to control other people's reactions to us. In that sense, humor becomes a form of people pleasing. There's nothing wrong with bringing joy and laughter but when a Comedian part jumps into action to "ease the tension" and thus, avoid conflict, then we can see how humor can act as a diversion from a potentially uncomfortable situation. Humor makes a great distraction.

Humor can also be a way to connect with others. Laughing together creates a bond of affection. Again, not a bad thing at all! But when your Comedian starts performing at the office or neighborhood barbecue, it's important to ask if that is a part's way of offering value for friendship rather than risk confirming an exile's fear of not being good enough, just as you are. You are worthy of love and belonging even if you aren't providing a steady stream of laughter.

Thoughts to ponder: Today's scripture contrasts the beauty of a "joyful heart" with a "crushed spirit [that] dries up the bones." What is driving your humor? Joy or fear?

SHAME, SHAME, GO AWAY

JESUS THEN BEGAN TO TEACH THEM THAT THE SON OF MAN MUST SUFFER MANY THINGS AND BE REJECTED BY THE ELDERS, THE CHIEF PRIESTS AND THE TEACHERS OF THE LAW, AND THAT HE MUST BE KILLED AND AFTER THREE DAYS RISE AGAIN. HE SPOKE PLAINLY ABOUT THIS, AND PETER TOOK HIM ASIDE AND BEGAN TO REBUKE HIM. BUT WHEN JESUS TURNED AND LOOKED AT HIS DISCIPLES, HE REBUKED PETER. "GET BEHIND ME, SATAN!" HE SAID. "YOU DO NOT HAVE IN MIND THE CONCERNS OF GOD, BUT MERELY HUMAN CONCERNS. MARK 8: 31-33

I'm so stupid.

I can't believe I did that. Again!

I'll never get it right.

If I just tried harder, I'd be a better [wife/husband, mother/father, worker, Christian, person...]

I'm fat.

I'm lazy.

I'm worthless.

I'm not good enough.

I've never met anyone who didn't use some form of internal shaming to attempt to correct behavior. A Shaming part will step in after other managers fail at something. Shame comes in to "clean up the mess" and, more importantly, to make sure it never happens again. (Even though it will.)

Shame does have a purpose. It combines guilt over doing something wrong with the fear of being cast out from a group or community so that we behave better and will be allowed to stay a member of the community. The act of shaming is an aspect of every known culture and it's an effective tool for shaping individuals into compliance with group norms. Society attempts to prevent chaos by threatening to reject those who don't conform.

Peter tried to use shame to correct Jesus. When Jesus was telling the disciples that he would soon be killed Peter pulled Jesus aside to rebuke him. This was mere moments after Peter had declared Jesus as the Christ, the Son of the living God. Peter was uncomfortable with what Jesus was telling him, so he tried to shame Jesus into being the kind of Messiah that Peter wanted him to be.

Jesus wasn't havin' it. He rebuked Peter and said, "Get behind me, Satan!" Jesus was not going to conform to the distorted image that Peter (or more likely a part of Peter) held. Jesus was also rebuking Satan, the Prince of Lies, who is always happy to let fear and negativity lead us astray.

While shame does serve a purpose in communal living, Jesus was comfortable rejecting undeserved shame.

Peter was probably very sincere in his attempt to protect Jesus. So are our internal protectors, including Shame. Sometimes we have to ask ourselves if a burdened part is acting like Peter. If so, we need to help that part release its burden of shame.

Thoughts to ponder: Do you have a misguided Shame part? How do these parts try to protect you?

MIRROR, MIRROR

YOU HAVE SET OUR INEQUITIES BEFORE YOU, OUR SECRET SINS IN THE LIGHT OF YOUR PRESENCE. PSALMS 90:8

We all wear a mask when we go out into the world. That mask depends on what you want the world to believe about you. Wearing a mask is neither a good thing nor a bad thing. It's just a human thing. It's a part. Often, the mask we attempt to wear is our idealized self—the person we *really* want to see in the mirror. The person we want to be once our mess is cleaned up and we do all the things we know we are supposed to do. The person we've always wanted to be. The person we want others to believe we are.

Sometimes this public part is so different from who we are—and who our Critics tell us we should be—that we end up feeling like a fraud. But the truth is that the Mask and the Critic are both just doing their best in their limited ways, to protect us from the shame or embarrassment of looking bad in others' eyes.

The Mask we put on is a part that is searching for acceptance and for a place to belong. It is aware that others judge and it's trying to protect us from being found wanting.

The problem with the Mask is that the donning of it immediately creates a secret of who we really are. And secrets feel sneaky. We start to feel fake.

Worse, if we have a part that believes the separation between who we want to be and who we really are is shameful, wearing the Mask will make us feel like a hypocrite. The Mask may feel like proof of our unworthiness.

There are three images of ourselves here: the person we are afraid we really are, the person we want to be, and the person others see.

Only God sees and knows us as we really, really, *really* are. Only God can see past our Mask, past our faulty beliefs to the vulnerable, broken, amazing, wonderful person we truly are. As scary as it feels to contemplate, God sees us wholly.

Thoughts to ponder: What do you want people to see when they interact with you? Are there aspects of yourself that you want to hide? How do you feel about the difference between who you are and who you wish you were? What are you afraid to let people see? What are you afraid to let God see?

KNOW AND BE KNOWN

THEN LEAVING HER WATER JAR, THE WOMAN WENT BACK TO TOWN AND SAID TO THE PEOPLE, "COME, SEE A MAN WHO TOLD ME EVERYTHING I EVER DID. COULD THIS BE THE MESSIAH?" THEY CAME OUT OF TOWN AND MADE THEIR WAY TOWARD HIM. JOHN 4:28-30

Our Worriers are some of the hardest working, most dedicated parts around. Their mission—think of *all* the things and solve *all* the problems before the problems even become problems. Their motto: No surprises = no mistakes.

Unfortunately, this attempt to be able to predict and circumvent the future forces our Worriers into constant, unrelenting feedback loops of thought. Usually at 3:00 a.m. Logic is futile.

Kind of. A direct assault using logic, usually coordinated by another desperate, overworked manager, rarely works. It seems like it should help, but parts are made of sterner stuff than mere logic.

What does work is compassion and understanding offered amid a relationship with Self and these parts. Being curious and asking questions to learn more about each part—both the Worrier and the Logical—is the place to start.

When Jesus met the Samaritan woman at the well, he told her how she could receive the living water that he alone offers. She didn't see how that was possible, but instead of trying to explain or persuade her, Jesus showed her that he knew her. He knew her history, her secrets, her shame. He knew her completely. Being known gave immediate assurance of Jesus' authority and swept away all of the woman's doubts. When we are known, fully known, it touches a place in our heart and we feel loved.

This is true for our parts as well as our whole self. When we sit with agitated parts and seek to know them, they feel comforted and will calm down. We need to form a warm and loving relationship with the parts that make up our inner world.

Thoughts to ponder: Sit quietly and remember a time when you felt truly seen and known. How did that feel? Is this an experience you are willing to offer your inner parts?

No Sleep for You!

All this I have spoken of while still with you. But the Advocate, the Holy Spirit, whom the Father will send in my name, will teach you all the things and remind you of everything I have said to you. Peace I leave with you; my peace I give you. I do not give to you as the world gives. Do not let your hearts be troubled and do not be afraid. John 11:25-27

My favorite "Seinfeld" episodes had a character called the Soup Nazi. If a customer broke one of the Soup Nazi's rules, they would hear the dreaded words, "No soup for you!" No amount of begging or pleading would induce the rigid chef to show mercy.

Insomnia can feel just as unreasonable and unrelenting. To relax, parts that keep us busy and distracted during the day are expected to set aside those strategies at night. That feels dangerous. The past and the present loom large in the dark stillness of the night. The act of falling asleep means lowering defenses, and making ourselves vulnerable. Protective parts don't like being vulnerable. Not at all.

The middle of the night seems to be a favored time amongst Worrier parts, too. That way they get your sole attention as they spin off reams of possibilities of things to go wrong in a desperate effort to solve the problem before it even exists. And don't forget Regret! Regretful parts thrive in the dark of night. That's when we get to play that game, "Why on earth did I SAY that?" or "What if I never get to [insert dream/goal here.]

It's easy to feel alone and ill-equipped in the night—cut off from even the support of our busy managers. It can be hard to remember that God and Self are always with us and they are eager to bring comfort and calm to our inner world.

Thoughts to ponder: Is there a part that is involved in keeping you from sleep? Get to know this part.

BACK TO THE PRESENT

YOU MAKE KNOWN TO ME THE PATH OF LIFE;
IN YOUR PRESENCE THERE IS FULLNESS OF
JOY, AT YOUR RIGHT HAND ARE PLEASURES
FOREVERMORE. PSALMS 16:11

When we worry about the future or ruminate on the past, we become disconnected from God's peace. C. S. Lewis had a wonderful observation about time. He said, "The Future is, of all things, least like Eternity. It is the most temporal (worldly as opposed to spiritual) part of time—for the Past is frozen and no longer flows and the Present is all lit up with eternal rays."

God is not limited to time as we know it. He is always Present. He is "I Am." When our wounded parts keep us preoccupied with things out of our control—the past or the future—we step out of connection with God and our own Self.

Many of our burdened parts struggle to trust any being, including themselves. Our Self and some of our parts may be able to rest in God's peace, but burdened parts... not so much. Building a safe relationship with them—Self to parts—will also open up opportunities for the part to be able to trust God.

Meditation is the practice of noticing and being in the present moment. Christian meditation can include pondering scripture, softening your heart, or simply sitting in delicious peace with our Creator.

Thoughts to ponder: How do the past or the future create obstacles for your ability to stay in God's peaceful present? Do you have burdened parts who are struggling with trust and/or reliance on God? How can you include a Christ-focused meditation practice in your communion with God?

BEHIND THE WALL

FOR YOU HAVE BEEN A DEFENSE FOR THE HELPLESS, A DEFENSE FOR THE NEEDY IN HIS DISTRESS, A REFUGE FROM THE STORM, A SHADE FROM THE HEAT; FOR THE BREATH OF THE RUTHLESS IS LIKE A RAINSTORM AGAINST A WALL. ISAIAH 25:4

Relationships can be scary and confusing. It's not surprising that our parts show up in big ways amid relationships. The more intimate the relationship, the more exposed we are, and the more skittish and reactive our parts get. Many people describe a "wall" that regulates intimacy.

Q: "What happens when someone gets too close?"

A: "A wall goes up."

Sound familiar? The Wall is a part that has been carefully constructed to keep others out and us, safely inside. Every subsequent hurt, every new betrayal, or broken promise simply adds another brick to the Wall.

The Wall believes that it is protecting you from relationship pain. There are valid reasons for its existence. When we have been betrayed, abused, abandoned, or neglected by a loved one who was supposed to be loyal, safe, reliable, and nurturing, then it's no surprise that a part will step up to protect us from being hurt that way again. Over time, the Wall gets thicker, deeper, taller. We put up signs. "No Entry!" "Trespassers Will Be Prosecuted!" "Beware of Dog!!"

It works. The Wall protects us as walls are supposed to do. But such stalwart protection comes at a price. It gets lonely behind the Wall. Boring, even. We are isolated and feel even more alone. We may even start to feel rejected or neglected by the people who haven't made it past the Wall or who, perhaps, gave up trying.

The Wall doesn't care that we feel lonely. It has one job, and it's going to do it. It's like... well... like talking to a brick wall. The Wall doesn't understand that most walls have doors or gates and maybe a window here and there. Other parts such as those in charge of relationships or who might be tired of being lonely get frustrated with the Wall but, again, the Wall is gonna do what the Wall is supposed to do.

The real problem is that God is supposed to be our wall of protection. People will fail us. Even the Wall will fail us at some point by either letting in someone who hurts us or by not letting in those who could help us. God is our one perfect defense.

Thoughts to ponder: Learn about your Wall. How long has the Wall been protecting you from more relationship harm? What is it afraid will happen if it lets people in?

Negative Reinforcement

A GENTLE ANSWER TURNS AWAY WRATH, BUT A HARSH WORD STIRS UP ANGER. PROV 15:1 THOSE WHO ARE KIND BENEFIT THEMSELVES, BUT THE CRUEL BRING RUIN ON THEMSELVES. PROV 11:17 GRACIOUS WORDS ARE A HONEYCOMB, SWEET TO THE SOUL AND HEALING TO THE BONES. PROV 16:24

I have never met anybody who doesn't have some kind of Inner Critic. Maybe God put one in everyone. If a part's mission has something to do with using negative self-talk as a way to make sure that you live up to high standards, then you can bet that part is an Inner Critic.

Inner Critics are dedicated to enforcing a certain code of conduct or belief system that they believe is necessary for survival. They are simply trying to help you be the best you that you can be. Unfortunately, some Inner Critics can be quite unkind about it. Unkindness often comes from fear, and that's typically what is pushing the Inner Critic. Fear that you are going to make a mistake. Fear that you are going to disappoint others or yourself. Fear of letting ourselves or others down. Fear of embarrassment or failure.

Burdened Inner Critics can be relentless. They have impossible standards. They show no mercy. They don't believe that mistakes are human; they believe that mistakes are sins.

Needless to say, Inner Critics are not very well-liked by either the inner world or the people in the outer world. How could they be? And yet, like all parts, their mission is to protect and to help, no matter what the cost. Frankly, the cost--the repercussions--isn't their problem.

The Inner Critic often, unknowingly, plays right into Satan's hand. Their negative and degrading self-talk creates fertile ground for the Liar. Not on purpose. They just can't consider the consequences.

Attempting to silence our Inner Critics (or any other part, for that matter) may work temporarily but without healing, they generally pop right back. They have squatters' rights. Challenging them rarely works. They aren't interested in reason. But what does work is a softer approach. Building trust. After all, the Bible tells us that gentleness and kindness are the answers for "turning away wrath," "nourishing your soul," and are "sweet and healthy."

Thoughts to ponder: How does your Inner Critic try to help you? What is it afraid will happen if you don't meet those high standards?

EXILES RE[PEAT] [PAIR] [DEEM] RELATIONSHIPS

THE THIEF COMES ONLY TO STEAL AND KILL AND DESTROY; I HAVE COME THAT THEY MAY HAVE LIFE, AND HAVE IT TO THE FULL. JOHN 10:10

Exiles carry the burdens of broken relationships. Bad things happen, often by people we are supposed to trust and depend on, and burdened exiles are born. That is to say, a formerly happy and healthy part responds to a trauma or a relationship injury by stepping in and absorbing the pain. It shoulders the burden. The exile learns that relationships are scary, treacherous, and painful.

Sadly, exiles are often driven to *repeat* relationships with people who remind them of those original broken connections. This is a misguided attempt to *repair* the broken pieces. To make everything all right again. These exiles crave *redemption*—a way back to feeling worthy of love. Unfortunately, because these "re-do" attempts usually involve equally damaged partners, the repair rarely works.

You cannot repair old traumas by repeating them.

You might be able to repair current relationships, though. Even those relationships you still have with the people who hurt you to begin with. Or not. Self can decide if that's a good idea or not.

Thankfully, the redemption of yourself or your parts doesn't require the original-wound person to cooperate or even participate in the repair work. Self and God are all that is necessary.

Thoughts to ponder: Are there relationships that you are trying to repair by repeating them? What would it feel like to let that go and open your heart to the redemption that God alone will bring?

RESENTMENT IS A CLUE

REMEMBER: WHOEVER SOWS SPARINGLY WILL ALSO REAP SPARINGLY, AND WHOEVER SOWS GENEROUSLY WILL ALSO REAP GENEROUSLY. EACH OF YOU SHOULD GIVE WHAT YOU HAVE DECIDED IN YOUR HEART TO GIVE, NOT RELUCTANTLY OR UNDER COMPULSION, FOR GOD LOVES A CHEERFUL GIVER. 2 COR 9:6-7

It feels good to help. There is absolutely nothing wrong with having a giving heart. We are even called upon to take care of one another. But sometimes we learn unhealthy lessons about giving. Maybe we learned about giving from our grandma who kept everyone clothed and fed. Maybe we learned about giving from taking care of a chronically sick parent. Maybe we learned about giving by watching a parent with their own Caretaking part wear themselves out taking care of their alcoholic spouse. Somewhere along the way some of us learned to "give 'til it hurts... then give some more."

There are a lot of roles that our parts can take on concerning giving: hero, rescuer, people-pleaser, caretaker, fixer. Strong people give. Loving people give. Where is the line between heartfelt giving and being taken advantage of? When does giving become a weakness for both giver and receiver?

One of the biggest red flags indicating unhealthy giving is resentment. Resentment (or its sibling, annoyance) is a complex emotion that involves a sense of unfairness or injury. Resentment is an emotional alert that your boundaries have been crossed in some way. It's a clue that you are ignoring something important, probably something to do with your values or sense of self.

Listen to the part of you that is expressing resentment. You might first have to work with another part that may have been trying to squelch the resentment or feels guilty about it. Parts have feelings about other parts.

It's my fault. I always let him get away with it.

If I do this, then maybe she will finally understand how much I care.

If I don't do this, nobody else will, and then where will she be?

Don't get me wrong. Sometimes giving is centered in love and an open heart. Celebrate that! But sometimes giving has more to do with burdened responsibility. Sometimes it might even be about control.

The Bible talks a lot about giving. 2 Corinthians 9:6-7 tells us that God loves a cheerful giver and when we give generously, we will also receive generously. But the next verse takes a look at our hearts. It says we should give "what we have decided to give in our hearts" making the act of giving both a head decision and a heart decision. It goes on to say that giving should not make us feel reluctant or coerced.

The important thing is to check your heart to see if it is aligned with godly reasons for giving and, if not, explore the feelings that a burdened giving part might be experiencing.

Thoughts to ponder: What lessons did you learn along the way about giving? What is in your heart when you give? Do you recognize resentment as an emotional alert that you might not be making a choice that aligns with your values?

None So Blind

Then Samson prayed to the Lord, "Sovereign Lord, remember me. Please, God, strengthen me just once more, and let me with one blow get revenge on the Philistines for my two eyes." Judges 16: 28

Blinders are leather flaps on a bridle that narrow a horse's view, cutting off peripheral (wider) vision. This keeps the horse from startling at objects and instinctively bolting away in fear. So, blinders were created as an inhibiting, protective measure.

Our burdened parts wear emotional blinders. Their solutions to traumatic or emotionally threatening events had one objective (survive) and to do so, they created an effective method for handling the difficulties they faced. Back then, this narrow-visioned approach was the best or only way they knew back then to protect themselves. What's more, at that time, their method worked. You survived. Because of that success, parts still use the same "tried and true" approach today *even if* this way now creates as many problems as it used to solve.

Samson is a great example of someone who used the same approach over and over again to his own detriment. Samson didn't like the hassle of conflict. He told lies or simply avoided the issue. If pushed into dealing with a problem, he would get enraged and violent. When Samson got involved with Delilah (who was working for the Philistines to try to discover Samson's secret to his strength), she kept up a steady campaign of whining and wheedling to get him to tell her his secret. Samson had to know what was happening, but he continued to hang out with her despite knowing that Delilah was betraying him. Several times, in fact. He took the easy way out and countered her nagging and attempts to manipulate him by making up stories about how he came to be so strong. Samson stayed in the relationship with Delilah even after she repeatedly proved her disloyalty.

This wasn't the first woman to wheedle information out of Samson, either. Apparently, a part of Samson was drawn to beautiful conniving women. Samson didn't learn his lesson and he remained blind to the unhealthy choices he made in his relationships. It wasn't until he was captured and literally blinded by the Philistines that he became desperate enough to turn to God in prayer. Only then was Samson able to acknowledge his dependence on God and allow Him to use Samson to find victory amid his greatest defeat. Despite an untold number of missed opportunities and poor choices, God still used Samson to deliver Israel from the Philistines.

Thoughts to ponder: What are some ways that your burdened parts keep you blinded? How did those "tried and true" methods of burdened parts help you survive back in the day? When did those approaches stop working? How do those formerly helpful methods create obstacles for you in the present day?

PEACE AT ALL COST

IF YOUR BROTHER OR SISTER SINS, GO AND POINT OUT THEIR FAULT JUST BETWEEN THE TWO OF YOU. IF THEY LISTEN TO YOU, YOU HAVE WON THEM OVER. MATT 18:15

Conflict is a fact of life. How (or if) we handle conflict depends on how we feel about it.

Avoiding, running away, or preemptively giving in are all tactics that a conflict-averse person will use, often at the expense of their own interests. "It's not worth the hassle" is a common rationale. There are indeed times when it's prudent to let an argument go but "pick your battles" does not mean avoiding *all* the battles.

Not liking conflict is not the same thing as fearing it. When fear is involved—whether it's fear of losing an argument and feeling stupid, fear of losing a relationship and feeling abandoned, or a learned trauma response – it's practically a guarantee that a troubled part is struggling to handle the situation in the only way they know how.

Many Christians avoid anger and conflict, believing that anger is un-Christian. But scripture shows us that both God and Jesus get angry. And both of them have dealt appropriately with those who expressed anger toward them. Jesus' very existence created a conflict with those who felt threatened by his message.

Like Jesus, our confident and centered Self doesn't avoid conflict and neither does it seek conflict out. Self has the confidence to set boundaries when necessary and Self knows how to be assertive without being aggressive.

Most of us know how we should respond to conflict but don't feel able to do so. We have to explore the part's learned response before we can change it.

Thoughts to ponder: How do you respond to conflict? Where did you learn to handle that particular way of dealing with anger and conflict? Why was it important to behave in those protective ways?

PERFECTLY PERFECT IN EVERY WAY

Therefore, in order to keep me from being conceited, I was given a thorn in my flesh, a messenger of Satan to torment me. Three times I pleaded with the Lord to take it away for me. But he said to me, "My grace is sufficient for you, for my power is made perfect in weakness." Therefore, I will boast all the more gladly about my weakness, so that Christ's power may rest on me. Cor 12:7-9

Perfection is an illusion. So why are so many of us convinced we must achieve it? The lure of perfection is grounded in the belief that if we can attain it, we won't suffer the crippling shame of making a mistake. No mistakes equals no regret.

Perfection is a myth. Western society has made an idol out of success and achievement. Many troubled manager parts use achievements as a way of racking up external validation in lieu of intrinsic self-worth. If you have an "I'm Not Good Enough" exile, being able to point to items checked off a To-Do list, goals that are met or surpassed, promotions, raises, etc. can serve as a kind of proof of value.

Perfection is a trap. We believe that if we can control our self, others, or our environment we can avoid the anxiety and shame that failure brings. The problem, of course, is that perfection is impossible so the pursuit of it is guaranteed to fail. Failure drives the perfectionist even harder in a vain attempt to achieve the impossible. The anxiety of trying to control against disappointment and failure results in creating a constant source of it.

Perfection is without mercy. Perfection is a tyrant. Strangely enough, there is peace in imperfection. When we humbly accept our own shortcomings, we can free our Perfectionist from that impossible task. That part can still help us to try our best, but we can mitigate its harshness and offer ourselves the grace to be human.

Thoughts to ponder: Are you ruled by a Perfectionist part? What is this part afraid will happen if you make a mistake? Where did this part learn to be afraid of making a mistake? Of imperfection? Of failure?

LEGACIES

Do not hold against us the sins of past generations; may your mercy come quickly to meet us, for we are in desperate need. Help us, God our Savior, for the glory of your name; deliver us and forgive our sins for your name's sake. Psalm 79:8-9

Money, land, names, traditions, recipes, furniture, jewelry—these are physical things that can be passed down, generation to generation. There are other things, less tangible but just as impactful, that can also be passed down. Things like parenting styles, addictions, illnesses (both physical and mental), traditions, cultural influences, worldviews, belief systems, and so on.

And let's not forget trauma.

Children learn to understand the world by observing and absorbing how their parents view the world. Children learn "truths" about how relationships work by observing their parents relating to each other and to others. Children learn to fear what their parents fear. When parts absorb traumatic lessons learned from their ancestors' experiences, they acquire legacy burdens. These parts become burdened with protecting us from experiences that we, personally, never lived through but which we learned to fear anyway.

Generational curses are types of legacy burdens.

Abraham and his family are good examples of those who struggled with legacy-burdened parts. Abraham lied about his relationship with Sarah, his wife and half-sister. It caused a big ruckus. Later, he told the same lie for the same reason and got the same results.

And guess what? Isaac, Abraham's son, told the same lie—that his wife Rebecca wasn't his wife but was only his sister. Isaac told this lie for the same reason (fear) and caused the same results (anger from a powerful ruler.)

Abraham's grandson Jacob also resorted to lying so that he could steal his brother Esau's birthright.

Lots of lies. *Generational* lies. Abraham passed on a type of behavior that consistently caused more problems than it solved. Generational curses or legacy burdens are passed down but once recognized can be broken. Through Jesus Christ, God provided the path to freedom from all sin. With his death, Jesus offers grace, forgiveness, and mercy.

Thoughts to ponder: What legacy burden might you be carrying? Who did you inherit this particular burden from?

TIME DOESN'T HEAL

Then I saw "a new heaven and a new earth," for the first heaven and the first earth had passed away, and there was no longer any sea. I saw the Holy City, the new Jerusalem, coming down out of heaven from God, prepared as a bride beautifully dressed for her husband. And I heard a loud voice from the throne saying, "Look! God's dwelling place is now among the people, and he will dwell with them. They will be his people, and God himself will be with them and be their God. He will wipe every tear from their eyes. There will be no more death or mourning or crying or pain, for the old order of things has passed away. Rev 21:1-4

Sorry. But time does not heal all wounds. We want the past to stay in the past, but it doesn't. We can't shove it away. We can't stuff it down. We can't just let it go. Whatever happened in the past taught a vulnerable part of you what it can expect from the world or relationships or how you should view yourself. That life lesson became part of your makeup. That doesn't mean you can't heal in those areas, but not by ignoring that the pain exists.

God is the source of all righteousness and justice. He alone has power over our past. Not by erasing the past but by redeeming us in the present and offering hope for the future.

Hager, a servant of Sarah, tried running away from her pain. During her escape, God met Hager and told her to return and submit to Sarah's authority. God understood her pain and understood her impulse to run from it. So, He came to her in the wilderness to comfort and encourage her. God gave Hager guidance which included directing her to face the problem.

God doesn't waste pain. He uses every part of us—including our own past—to further His purpose, which is to make us more like Christ in every way. He is preparing us for a time when all suffering will truly be wiped away and we will dwell, pain-free, in His presence forever.

Thoughts to ponder: Have you found yourself fighting to keep the past in the past? What is God asking you to face? Is it possible that God wants to use your suffering in some way?

THE GOOD, THE BAD, & THE UGLY

For while we were still weak, at the right time Christ died for the ungodly. For one will scarcely die for a righteous person--though perhaps for a good person one would dare even to die but God shows his love for us in that while we were still sinners, Christ died for us. Romans 5: 6-8

It's common to regard our parts in terms of good or bad. Our managers are the easiest to like. Their jobs are to push us into being the ideal of who we want to be. Managers embrace the virtues of hard work, loyalty, organization, ambition, cleanliness, and so on. Managers are "good."

Firefighters, on the absolute other hand, can seem like troublemakers. They tend to create more problems than they solve and a lot of their "solutions" are highly questionable. Maybe even sinful. So, we often don't like our firefighters. Firefighters are "bad."

And exiles? Those pain-filled, stuffed down, silenced Untouchables? They are seen as weak and useless. Rejects. A complete waste of time. Exiles are all too easy to hate. Exiles disgust us. Exiles frighten us so we shove them away. Exiles are "ugly."

But aren't all parts supposed to be welcome? "Welcome" means more than just merely tolerating the presence of someone. Welcoming is a warm, open-hearted act of bringing another being into our circle and making them comfortable. Welcoming means acknowledging that someone belongs in our space or community. We are saying, "You belong and we're glad you're here!"

Welcoming parts means remembering that they are us and we are them. We are designed by God, in His image. Loved so completely that God sent part of himself, his son Jesus, to die for us. Because of Jesus' sacrifice, it's now possible for us to truly belong to God as His children.

Thoughts to ponder: Are there parts that you have been trying to cast out or shut down? Do you favor some parts more than others?

BUSY, BUSY, BUSY

The Lord said, "Go out and stand on the mountain in the presence of the Lord, for the Lord is about to pass by." Then a great and powerful wind toward the mountains apart and shattered the rocks before the Lord, but the Lord was not in the wind. After the wind, there was an earthquake, but the Lord was not in the earthquake. After the earthquake came a fire, but the Lord was not in the fire. And after the fire came a gentle whisper. When Elijah heard it, he pulled his cloak over his face and went out and stood at the mouth of the cave. Then a voice said to him, "What are you doing here, Elijah?" 1 Kings 19:11-13

Do you have a part that keeps you busy all the time? Having a Busy part helps us feel valued by being productive. This part may push us to achieve and succeed.

Busy parts give us clear and visible results. Best of all, with all of the tasks, projects, and errands that the Busy part signs us up for, we don't have time to stop and think. Or, even more frightening, stop and *feel*.

Busy parts get an awful lot done, but they are not so good at leaving time to *connect* with others. It can be lonely being Busy.

And, of course, there is no time to simply enjoy the moment. Truly enjoying something—a laugh, a delicious meal, a sunset—means taking a break from being so busy, and Busy parts don't know how to let that happen. For them, slowing down means risking an exile accidentally getting loose. For a Busy part, that's a great big nope!

Busy parts do not know how to rest. That's the very opposite of their job, after all. There is no peace for the Busy. No quiet time to tend to one's Self. Unfortunately, even when Busy is doing good things like serving at a church, volunteering at school, tackling the clutter that's piled up in the closet, not allowing time to rest will likely leave us feeling isolated and disconnected from our loved ones, our Self, and even God.

God speaks to us in the still moments. God came to Elijah, not in the roar of the wind or the earthquake or the fire but in the soft silence following the uproar. God whispers gently in a "small, still voice." If we are distracted or consumed with producing, we simply will not hear His gentle voice.

Thoughts to ponder: What thoughts or emotions do you feel when you think about sitting quietly with the Lord? Is there a part of you that is afraid of slowing down? What drives your Busy parts?

THE SCARIEST OF THEM ALL

PEACE I LEAVE WITH YOU; MY PEACE I GIVE TO YOU. NOT AS THE WORLD GIVES DO I GIVE TO YOU. LET NOT YOUR HEARTS BE TROUBLED, NEITHER LET THEM BE AFRAID. JOHN 14:27

Some things are hard to talk about. Some things are hard even to admit to ourselves. Things like suicidal thoughts or attempts. Self-harm, like cutting, pulling out your hair, scratching yourself, binging, or vomiting, etc. are dark secrets.

If all parts are welcome, how do we go about accepting the firefighters who embrace the possibility that ending our life is an acceptable last resort? How do we admit that the Self-Harm part makes us feel nothing and alive all at the same time? What possible good comes from these extreme self-destructive parts?

Start there with that question. What possible good...?

Firefighters have one purpose—numb the pain. They only emerge when managers fail to keep the exile from being triggered, thus flooding us with their raw overwhelming pain. Their willingness to self-destruct rather than allow us to face the pain is the very height of irony. Firefighters are the psychological equivalent of "cutting off your nose to spite your face."

Another irony is that it is often the fear of impulsive and seemingly out-of-control firefighters that eventually brings us to the point of seeking help. Managers perpetuate denial. Firefighters force us to admit that we indeed have a problem.

Understanding the extremes our firefighters are willing to go to in order to protect us from overwhelming pain is the first step in softening our hearts towards them. Remember: softening doesn't mean approving. It doesn't mean surrendering to self-destructive impulses, either. Love, not hate, brings healing and wholeness.

Thoughts to ponder: Reflect on your firefighters' intentions. How are they helping you avoid emotional pain? How do you feel toward your firefighter?

LEAVE BEFORE YOU'RE LEFT

CAN A MOTHER FORGET THE BABY AT HER BREAST AND HAVE NO COMPASSION FOR THE CHILD SHE HAS BORNE? THOUGH SHE MAY FORGET, I WILL NOT FORGET YOU! SEE, I HAVE ENGRAVED YOU ON THE PALMS OF MY HANDS; YOUR WALLS ARE EVER BEFORE ME. YOUR CHILDREN HASTEN BACK, AND THOSE WHO LEAD YOU WASTE DEPART FROM YOU. ISAIAH 49: 15-17

Leave before you're left. Hurt, agony, and betrayal... sounds like a country-western song, doesn't it? Parts that fear abandonment often use this technique to avoid rejection.

If the very possibility of rejection is too scary to live with, a part may dedicate itself to preemptively pulling away from intimate relationships to protect against being abandoned. After all, you can't be rejected if you leave first. You can't be abandoned if you are already gone. Yet when someone harbors a deep desire for connection, this approach is distinctly unhelpful. However, as a protection against that particular pain that comes from being rejected, there is a certain rationale to the method.

Leaving before we are left also works in situations that might expose us to the risk of failure. If we do a lousy job which, not surprisingly, ends up being rejected, at least it wasn't our best effort that was found wanting. If you never really try, it's not really you—the you that matters—that fails. It's the part that didn't try hard enough that failed and, frankly, that part doesn't care about failure, in that sense. If it keeps you from being rejected, that counts as a win. That part will have done its job.

At the heart of these self-sabotaging reactions is fear. Abandonment leaves an emotional and spiritual imprint on our souls.

Being left makes us believe that we were unworthy of being loved in the first place. This is the biggest, most destructive lie of the Enemy of all. Because we have *never* not been loved by God. Before we existed, He loved us. He loves us all through every moment of every day since the beginning of ever. God will never stop loving us.

God. Loves. You.

Thoughts to ponder: Has a part of you been so afraid of being abandoned that you sabotaged a relationship?

THE ONES WE HAVE TO HATE

I CARE VERY LITTLE IF I AM JUDGED BY YOU OR BY ANY HUMAN COURT; INDEED, I DO NOT EVEN JUDGE MYSELF. MY CONSCIENCE IS CLEAR, BUT THAT DOES NOT MAKE ME INNOCENT. IT IS THE LORD WHO JUDGES ME. THEREFORE, JUDGE NOTHING BEFORE THE APPOINTED TIME; WAIT UNTIL THE LORD COMES. HE WILL BRING TO LIGHT WHAT IS HIDDEN IN DARKNESS AND WILL EXPOSE THE MOTIVES OF THE HEART. AT THAT TIME EACH WILL RECEIVE THEIR PRAISE FROM GOD. 1 COR 4:3-5

It's all about the exiles. All of the energy, all of the effort, all of the work—it's all designed to protect the exiles. Protect and silence.

Managers stuff the feelings down. Firefighters distract or numb. But these behaviors are all about keeping the pain of the exiles from reigniting and coming to life again.

Exiles are the secrets. Unfortunately, keeping them in the dark, isolated, and hidden, increases their negative energy and fosters shame. Exiles are a state of being. Their existence is rooted in their belief that they are unworthy, unlovable, or are somehow permanately broken. The attempts to stuff them down or shove them away only give power to these lies of the Enemy.

Exiles react to this treatment the same way anybody else would. Stuffing down or boxing them up makes exiles feel trapped and suffocated. They have no voice. They are powerless captives. They are the sum of our rejections.

Sadly, over time we become the ones abandoning these parts of ourselves.

Allowing exiles to step into the light takes a lot of courage and an understanding that God is with us every step of the way. Our worth is rooted in God, not in whatever lies the world or the Enemy has made us believe.

Thoughts to ponder: How do you feel toward your exiles? Are you ready to offer love and mercy to these hurting little ones?

Leave the Past in the Past

Then Joseph could no longer control himself before all his attendants, and he cried out, "Have everyone leave my presence!" So, there was no one with Joseph when he made himself known to his brothers. And he wept so loudly that the Egyptians heard him, and Pharaoh's household heard all about it. Then Joseph said to his brothers, "Come close to me." When they had done so, he said, "I am your brother Joseph, the one you sold into Egypt! And now, do not be distressed and do not be angry with yourselves for selling me here, because it was to save lives that God sent me ahead of you." Gen 45:1-2, 4-5

How many times have you said to yourself, "That was then, this is now. Just forget about it"? Or been told to "leave the past in the past." Or, best of all, "just let it go."

Has that ever worked? I mean, *ever*? Our brains are simply not designed to forget traumatic events or harmful lessons. Frankly, that would be dumb.

Our brains have been specifically designed to recognize the critical information that the memories of traumatic events hold. During life- or soul-threatening experiences, the brain immediately sets up systems to 1) be on alert for similar situations and 2) use what worked in the past to deal with the current (similar) problem. Unfortunately, the things that worked in the past (AKA those very things that allowed us to survive) may be less than helpful in the present.

Our brains are also designed to search for familiar patterns in relationships and environments. Even if we consciously recognize the unhealthiness of some of these familiar patterns we are drawn to them precisely *because* of that familiarity. This inclination toward the familiar helps explain why we may seem to repeat unhealthy or even abusive relationships, and we don't understand why. Ignoring the past will lead us to repeat it.

Joseph, son of Jacob, understood trauma. His jealous brothers plotted to kill him. Instead, they tossed him into a pit and then sold him as a slave. Later, Joseph had the opportunity to revenge himself on his brothers. Although Joseph didn't disclose who he was to his brothers right away, he did take time to step away and weep. Joseph was fully in touch with the memory of his treatment and with the loss and pain that the betrayal of his brothers had cost him. He didn't run away from the pain. But neither did he stay stuck in it.

Thoughts to ponder: Have you discovered unhealthy patterns in your relationships? What "life lessons" do your difficult memories carry for you?

FATALLY DAMAGED, PERMANENTLY BROKEN

FOR GOD SO LOVED THE WORLD THAT HE GAVE HIS ONE AND ONLY SON, THAT WHOEVER BELIEVES IN HIM SHALL NOT PERISH BUT HAVE ETERNAL LIFE. FOR GOD DID NOT SEND HIS SON INTO THE WORLD TO CONDEMN THE WORLD, BUT TO SAVE THE WORLD THROUGH HIM. JOHN 3:16-17

Children assume responsibility for the brokenness they are born into. How could they not? The alternative is to believe that our parents—the very people our survival depends upon—are unsafe and/or incapable of loving us. That is simply too scary to contemplate. So, as children, we decide that we are the ones that are somehow and for always broken. Parts get burdened. This is the genesis of every exile and the wellspring of unhealthy shame.

Your Self knows that this belief is a lie, but the exile believes it wholeheartedly. And, make no mistake, Satan will certainly use this belief against you.

The Bible is full of broken people. Sometimes it almost seems like God goes out of His way to pick the most unlikely persons to do His will. Abraham was too old and tended to lie his way out of tricky situations. Elijah was suicidal. Moses was insecure and also killed a man. Gideon was afraid. Sampson, a womanizer with anger issues. Rahab, a prostitute. Even the men Jesus chose for his inner circle had their issues with greed, jealousy, and impulsiveness.

Aside from Jesus, there is not one human who is capable of being worthy of God. And yet, He loves us. Loves us to pieces. God loves the undeserved, unreservedly.

Thoughts to ponder: Do you have a part that believes, despite all logic and faith, that you are somehow inherently unlovable or without real value?

MANAGER FEARS

IF I SPEAK IN THE TONGUES OF MEN OR OF ANGELS, BUT DO NOT HAVE LOVE, I AM ONLY A RESOUNDING GONG OR A CLANGING CYMBAL. IF I HAVE THE GIFT OF PROPHECY AND CAN FATHOM ALL MYSTERIES AND ALL KNOWLEDGE, AND IF I HAVE A FAITH THAT CAN MOVE MOUNTAINS, BUT DO NOT HAVE LOVE, I AM NOTHING. IF I GIVE ALL I POSSESS TO THE POOR AND GIVE OVER MY BODY TO HARDSHIP THAT I MAY BOAST, BUT DO NOT HAVE LOVE, I GAIN NOTHING. 1 COR: 13: 1-3

Burdened parts are afraid.

Mostly they fear being overwhelmed with pain from the exiles. Their reason for existence is solely for that. But managers are afraid of other things, too. Most of these fears can ultimately be traced back to an exile's traumatic experience(s) but when we are getting to know our protective parts, it's important to recognize that each of them has specific jobs which come with specific fears. A Perfectionist is afraid of making mistakes. A People-Pleaser fears making someone angry. A Wall fears betrayal. A Suicide part is terrified of unrelenting suffering.

These unique fears drive our managers' and firefighters' behaviors. When we learn what these fears are and explore how and why they developed, our parts feel seen. They are still locked into their protective role but, through Self, our being curious about what drives them gives these protectors their first glimpse at what building a relationship with us might offer. They are no longer alone. They feel loved. They feel safe.

Parts will respond to Self's willingness to bear witness to their greatest fears and darkest secrets with a sigh of relief and a feeling of gratitude. Feeling safe and loved creates a sense of peace throughout the whole person.

To be seen is to be loved, feeling loved brings peace. Without love, we are nothing.

Thoughts to ponder: Read the scripture as if from the perspective of one of your parts. See how it sits with them. Are they able to take in the message of love? If not, explore with them whatever is preventing them from feeling loved.

Members of the Body

Now there are varieties of gifts, but the same Spirit; and there are varieties of service, but the same Lord; and there are varieties of activities, but it is the same God who empowers them all in everyone. To each is given the manifestation of the Spirit for the common good. For to one is given through the Spirit the utterance of wisdom, and to another the utterance of knowledge according to the same Spirit, to another faith by the same Spirit, to another gifts of healing by the one Spirit, to another the working of miracles, to another prophecy, to another the ability to distinguish between spirits, to another various kinds of tongues, to another the interpretation of tongues. All these are empowered by one and the same Spirit, who apportions to each one

> INDIVIDUALLY AS HE WILLS. FOR JUST AS THE BODY IS ONE AND HAS MANY MEMBERS, AND ALL THE MEMBERS OF THE BODY, THOUGH MANY, ARE ONE BODY, SO IT IS WITH CHRIST. FOR BY ONE SPIRIT WE WERE ALL BAPTIZED INTO ONE BODY—JEWS OR GREEKS, SLAVES OR FREE—AND ALL WERE MADE TO DRINK OF ONE SPIRIT. 1 COR 12:4-14

Self is not better than the parts. We do want to have easier and deeper access to Self, but we are naturally made to have parts. We need them. They are us. Being in Self all of the time is not the goal. In fact, there is no end goal. If you, in any way, have the thought that always being in Self is how you "should be," then that is very likely a Perfectionist at work. In the same way, a leader of a team is not the most important player because where would the leader be without the team? Where would Self be without the parts?

Chapter Twelve in First Corinthians explores the way to celebrate the diversity of our having different spiritual gifts and different roles in the Church.

Being led by the Holy Spirit means celebrating these differences and putting each gift in service to the Lord. The members of a church have specialized gifts and contribute to the health of the church in different ways but are all guided by the Holy Spirit.

God designed our physical bodies to have different parts that have specific purposes in order to make a healthy functioning body guided by one central nervous system. Likewise, God designed us with different parts of personality that have different jobs, and each contributes to our emotional health and is to be led by our Self.

Thoughts to ponder: How do your parts serve you? How might they serve God?

BLENDED, NOT STIRRED

So I say, walk by the Spirit, and you will not gratify the desires of the flesh. For the flesh desires what is contrary to the Spirit, and the Spirit what is contrary to the flesh. They are in conflict with each other, so that you are not to do whatever you want. But if you are led by the Spirit, you are not under the law. Gal 5: 16-18

In IFS, blending is a process that means a part has been fully triggered and, in the chaos of the intense emotions, you don't seem to have any access to Self. Essentially, something happened and a part is re-living the agony of the original wounding. The part is so immersed in the original wound that it doesn't realize that the wound isn't actually happening in the present moment. The pain is as fresh and impactful as when the blow was first dealt. Traumatic memories have no sense of time passing. (That's why time can't heal them.)

We can only work with parts if we are in or have access to Self. Self centers us in an oasis of calm, curiosity, compassion, clarity, etc. Healing requires access to this centered Self, which likewise has access to the Holy Spirit.

Blending with these intense, seemingly uncontrollable emotions is not a pleasant experience. It often leaves us feeling like we've just been hijacked by an irrational, panicking toddler. This is true. That's exactly what happened.

The loss of control in those moments is bewildering. And the aftermath of that hijacking is shame and embarrassment. The fact that "it" happened again, even after we promised ourselves and others that such a thing would never happen again.

Recognizing that a troubled part "jumped into the driver's seat" is the first step toward creating a space between that part and Self. Simply noticing. Noticing is an act that automatically creates a dual awareness; there is a Noticer (Self, hopefully) and a part being noticed. Noticing allows us to begin the process of creating separation between a highly triggered part and the calm, centered Self that we all have.

Once you unblend, you will be able to reflect on what happened and explore the role that parts played in the outburst.

Thoughts to ponder: What does it feel like to you when you are blended with a triggered part? What do other people see? How do you feel in the aftermath?

BY GOD'S DESIGN

FOR YOU FORMED MY INWARD PARTS; YOU KNITTED ME TOGETHER IN MY MOTHER'S WOMB. I PRAISE YOU, FOR I AM FEARFULLY AND WONDERFULLY MADE. WONDERFUL ARE YOUR WORKS; MY SOUL KNOWS IT VERY WELL. MY FRAME WAS NOT HIDDEN FROM YOU, WHEN I WAS BEING MADE IN SECRET, INTRICATELY WOVEN IN THE DEPTHS OF THE EARTH. YOUR EYES SAW MY UNFORMED SUBSTANCE; IN YOUR BOOK WERE WRITTEN, EVERY ONE OF THEM, THE DAYS THAT WERE FORMED FOR ME, WHEN AS YET THERE WAS NONE OF THEM. PSALM 139: 13-16

There is only one you. You are the only you that there ever has been or ever will be. You are a discrete and utterly unique unit in the limitless expanse of infinity. No matter how many people have ever existed before, during, or after you exist, there is only one you. You are specifically designed by God to be you. Father Greg Boyle, a Jesuit priest who founded Homeboy Industries, the world's largest gang intervention and rehabilitation program, and former pastor of Dolores Mission Church in Los Angeles said, "You want people to recognize the truth of who they are—that they are exactly what God had in mind when God made them."

There is no denying that the tragedies and ugliness of this broken world affect who we become. Parts become burdened. At these times, the Self feels distant. Self—our soul—has not been destroyed as some might fear, but our access to the calm center of our being may, at times, become obscured. Burdened parts take on the onerous task of dealing with the pain of life. Soon we feel more and more distant from our Self and from God.

But we are still His—even when we feel adrift. His design has not been altered. It's been shielded. The Self is still there, waiting to emerge and reengage, as soon as we turn toward it. Just as God is.

Sometimes there is a need for addressing and healing the brokenness. It is not a simple process but the journey toward reconnection will teach us new and important things about our Self, our parts, and God.

Thoughts to ponder: What do you think God had in mind when He designed *you*?

SUFFER TOGETHER

A MAN WITH LEPROSY CAME AND KNELT BEFORE JESUS AND SAID, "LORD, IF YOU ARE WILLING, YOU CAN MAKE ME CLEAN." JESUS REACHED OUT HIS HAND AND TOUCHED THE MAN. "I AM WILLING," HE SAID. "BE CLEAN!" IMMEDIATELY, HE WAS HEALED FROM LEPROSY.
MATT 8:2-3

Compassion is one of several characteristics of Self. Compassion means "to suffer together." It is the flowing of love that is elicited in response to another's pain. Compassion connects us. When a person or part that is in pain feels this loving connection, they no longer feel alone. This is the fertile ground where healing takes place.

Jesus touched lepers. He didn't need to. He could just as easily have healed them with a word, but compassion moved him to "suffer with." To demonstrably show that he was meeting more than their medical needs. Jesus' touch delivered more than physical healing. Jesus established a physical connection to people who had been starved for touch. Skin-upon-skin closeness with those who had been rejected from all human society because of their illness. The "untouchables."

Jesus' touch erased shame. He demonstrated the value and acceptance of people who just moments before encountering him were forced to shout "Unclean! Unclean!" to warn everyone to back away. Lepers were threats. They were the living dead.

How they must have hated themselves, too!

Jesus knew how damaging self-loathing and shame are, and he took pains to make sure that this healing moment included far more than physical relief. His compassion was for the whole person, inside and out.

As Christians' we know that feeling compassion for others is kind of a big deal. We learn that lesson pretty early on. But what about showing compassion for ourselves? Why is it so difficult to extend that same compassion for the mistakes or falls from grace that *we* make?

Thoughts to ponder: How would your life change if you were as kind and compassionate to yourself (your parts) as you are to others?

OPEN HEARTS

CLEANSE ME WITH HYSSOP, AND I WILL BE CLEAN; WASH ME, AND I WILL BE WHITER THAN SNOW. LET ME HEAR JOY AND GLADNESS; LET THE BONES YOU HAVE CRUSHED REJOICE. HIDE AWAY YOUR FACE FROM MY SINS AND BLOT OUT ALL MY INIQUITY. CREATE IN ME A PURE HEART, O GOD, AND RENEW A STEADFAST SPIRIT WITHIN ME. DO NOT CAST ME FROM YOUR PRESENCE OR TAKE YOUR HOLY SPIRIT FROM ME. RESTORE ME TO THE JOY OF YOUR SALVATION AND GRANT ME A WILLING SPIRIT, TO SUSTAIN ME. PSALM 51: 7-12

Compassion means having an "openhearted presence without the desire to fix or control." Let's break that down: *openhearted*. What does it mean to have an open heart? Having an open heart means holding our inclinations to judge or be critical in suspension. That's not easy. It may involve working with parts. Open hearted is a welcoming position.

And then: *presence*. Being present. Being attentive to the other person. Being *with* them. Our modern-day lives are so hectic and harried that being present with our Self or other people or even the Holy Spirit often eludes us. We have to learn how to be in the moment, fully present, and available to the NOW experience. A good reminder of this mindset is found in God's naming of Himself as "I Am."

And finally: *without the desire to fix or control.* Whoa. But isn't fixing a way of helping? Won't fixing the problem take away the suffering?

As soon as you start to concentrate on the problem you are taking your attention off of the other person. Your involvement gets tangled up with fixing and solving and you are no longer in Self. A part has taken over—albeit with good intentions—to relieve your anxiety about being in the presence of suffering and it has taken you out of Self. You are no longer offering compassion, you are offering a solution. A solution is nice, but it's not compassion and therefore, not healing.

When I'm suffering, I often want God to simply take the problem away. Fix it. Rarely does He do so. And yet—God is a compassionate and gracious God. He is ready—eager! —to sit and suffer with us. The God of the universe is open-hearted. He is always present as He exists outside of the restrictions of time. God doesn't just hand over a solution to the pain we are in, He offers comfort and healing within the safety of His holy presence.

Jesus is the literal embodiment of compassion. He came to be *with us*. To sit and suffer *with us*. To die *for us*.

Thoughts to ponder: What part(s) does someone else's suffering bring up in you? How do these parts react when they are needed to witness another's pain?

IT HAPPENED

When they had finished breakfast, Jesus said to Simon Peter, "Simon, son of John, do you love me more than these?" He said to him, "Yes, Lord; you know that I love you." He said to him, "Feed my lambs." He said to him a second time, "Simon, son of John, do you love me?" He said to him, "Yes, Lord; you know that I love you." He said to him, "Tend my sheep." He said to him the third time, "Simon, son of John, do you love me?" Peter was grieved because he said to him the third time, "Do you love me?" and he said to him, "Lord, you know everything; you know that I love you." Jesus said to him, "Feed my sheep. Truly, truly, I say to you, when you were young, you used to dress yourself and walk wherever you wanted, but when you are old, you will stretch out your hands, and another will dress you and carry you where you

DO NOT WANT TO GO." (THIS HE SAID TO SHOW BY WHAT KIND OF DEATH HE WAS TO GLORIFY GOD.) AND AFTER SAYING THIS HE SAID TO HIM, "FOLLOW ME." JOHN 21:15-19

Somebody hurt you. It is okay to acknowledge that. Some Christians struggle with this. We don't have to feel guilty for recognizing that someone caused us pain. It's not about blaming them. It's not "being ungrateful" for other things they might have done right. It's not whining or selfish or unforgiving to acknowledge that you were hurt. It doesn't matter that the person who hurt you may have or may still love you. It doesn't matter that the person who hurt you may have been going through their own problems or may have never been taught how to love or how to deal with their stress or anger. It also doesn't matter if others in the world may have been hurt worse than you have been.

Acknowledging that you were hurt is about facing the reality that it happened, admitting it wasn't okay that it happened, and knowing that you have a right to feel what you feel about the experience. You cannot heal what you will not acknowledge.

When Jesus appeared to the disciples after his resurrection, he waited until after they had eaten together before turning to Peter and asking him if he (Peter) loved Jesus. Peter said he did. Then Jesus asked Peter two more times whether Peter did, indeed, love Jesus.

It must have occurred to Peter that this interaction mirrored the three times Peter had denied Jesus at the crucifixion. Jesus didn't ignore the fact that Peter had hurt him. Bringing the issue up to Peter was the only way that healing the relationship could begin. Talking about it allowed Peter to repent and reconnect. Peter could now move past his shame.

Thoughts to ponder: Do you pretend to yourself or others that the hurt you have experienced doesn't really hurt? Doesn't really matter? How might shame have impacted Peter's ability to minister and become the "rock upon which the Church could be built?"

Martha, Martha, Martha

Now as they went on their way, Jesus entered a village. And a woman named Martha welcomed him into her house. And she had a sister called Mary, who sat at the Lord's feet and listened to his teaching. But Martha was distracted with much serving. And she went up to him and said, "Lord, do you not care that my sister has left me to serve alone? Tell her then to help me." But the Lord answered her, "Martha, Martha, you are anxious and troubled about many things, but one thing is necessary. Mary has chosen the good portion, which will not be taken away from her.
Luke 10: 38-42

Some parts are so good at being in charge that they mimic the Self. It can be hard to tease out a manager who works so hard for the betterment of the whole person that even it believes it's the Self. Self-like parts can even have good ideas about wellness and self-care. They learn what works, after all. So how can we tell when we are truly in Self or when a self-like part is operating?

One of the biggest clues is that parts have an agenda and Self doesn't. Parts are concerned with doing or achieving; Self, with being. Parts do. Self is.

The danger in being led by self-like parts is that self-improvement can become an idol just as easily as any other "feel-good" activity. When this happens, prayers become rote, scripture feels stale, and service work breeds resentment.

When Jesus visited Mary and Martha, Mary was content to sit at Jesus' feet and bask in his presence. Martha had things to do. She bustled about, focused intently on serving the Lord. She wanted to please. She wanted to do the right thing. She wanted to show honor and love. That Martha felt correct in her attitude (and thus believed she was in Self) becomes apparent when Martha turns to Jesus and asks him to step in. Martha wanted Jesus to set Mary straight.

But it wasn't Mary who was out of balance.

Jesus told Martha that she was too worried about unimportant things. She had her priorities mixed up.

I can only imagine how confused Martha must have been at Jesus' response. She probably had to pray on that for a bit. Mull it over. Sort through the hurt feelings that got stirred up when she was chastised. Even if he was gentle about it. Even if it was for her own good.

Martha had to look deep inside in order to figure out what was going on in there. She had parts that had acted out of a set of beliefs that had been instilled in her. Martha had parts that jumped up to do the hard work, focused on following the rules, and desperately wanted by her acts of love to be found acceptable. Maybe having the Messiah over for dinner stirred up a lot of anxiety, pushing her out of Self. Who wouldn't be nervous?

But Jesus knows our hearts. He knew Martha's, too, and he knew she was not being led by her Self or the Spirit. She was caught up in the uncharitable thoughts in her head as she rushed around serving Jesus and his crew while "lazy" Mary sat on the ground!

Thoughts to ponder: How might you have felt if you were Martha? Do you have parts that "get lost in the work?" What did your family teach you about serving others?

RISKY BUSINESS

For the word of the Lord is right and true; he is faithful in all he does. The Lord loves righteousness and justice; the earth is full of his unfailing love.
Psalm 33: 4-5

When we begin a relationship, it does not make sense to trust the other person with all of our vulnerabilities. Not at first. We simply don't know them well enough to know if they are safe. Similarly, it may take time for parts to trust the Self. They have been betrayed, abused, and abandoned. Some may even feel like the Self left them to do all the dirty work.

Trust is a choice. It is both an action and a leap of faith. When someone asks us to trust them, they are asking us to risk getting hurt again. Earning trust from a person or part that has been deeply wounded is an honor that is not—and shouldn't be—bestowed lightly. Protective parts have the duty to protect their more vulnerable, wounded comrades. Trust is risky.

One of the trickier aspects of being in a relationship of any kind is that it is inevitable that the other person will eventually betray or wound us, somehow, some way. And we, them. Because we are human. The questions then become *should* we trust them again and *can* we trust them again? The first question has to do with the wisdom of trusting the person after a betrayal or wound. This has to do with their character and the likelihood of repeating errors of judgment. Factors like, has this happened before, did the other person accept accountability for the hurt they caused, are they repentant?

The latter question has to do with whether we have parts that will impede our ability to take the risk of getting hurt again. *Can* we trust again usually involves parts and whether they will permit vulnerability again. Sometimes a part will say, "Nope. Not going to risk it again." In that case, we need to help this part unburden itself of the wound that was caused. Mind you, that doesn't mean we don't heed that part's warning. Having the capacity to trust doesn't automatically mean we should go about completely unguarded.

We can run into this part in our relationship with God, too. In His case, His trustworthiness is not in question because God is holy and without fault. He never owes us an apology. Still, we may have a part or parts that struggle with trusting God. We will need to help the part(s) that are struggling with trust to open up about their experience and fears.

Taking time in solitude with God may be what is needed. Pray for or help the part pray to God. Let it be honest about how it feels. God can take it.

Thoughts to ponder: What parts are involved in your ability to trust others? What have your past experiences taught your parts about trusting others? About trusting your Self? About trusting God?

FREELY GIVEN

FOR IT IS BY GRACE YOU HAVE BEEN SAVED, THROUGH FAITH—AND THIS IS NOT FROM YOURSELVES, IT IS A GIFT FROM GOD—NOT BY WORKS, SO THAT NO ONE CAN BOAST. EPH 2: 8-9

Jesus welcomes everyone and accepts everyone no matter how great a sinner we may be. This acceptance from Jesus comes from our acceptance of Him and His sacrifice. Easy peasy, right?

Well... not so much.

When I think about Jesus nailed to the cross for me, to lift my sins and burdens from my shoulders for no good reason other than that God loves me, I go through a wide range of emotions. Sadness, that he should have to sacrifice himself. Anger at those who drove iron spikes through his wrists and feet. Horror that it was *my* sins, my humanness, which pinned him to the cross. Awe, that anyone could love me to that extent. Shame, that someone needed to.

It boggles the mind that instead of damnation we are instead brought into the loving embrace of the Creator of the universes. A part of me knows that I don't—I really don't—deserve grace. It seems unfair. Shouldn't we have to follow the rules to earn the reward? Frankly, this part knows it's getting away with something completely undeserved.

Justice and retribution seem to fill a primitive sense of fairness. Wrongs should get punished. Good behavior, rewarded. It just feels right, but mostly only when we are the ones who have been wronged or slighted.

Maybe accepting grace for our sins *without fully understanding* what it is is the beginning of faith.

Thoughts to ponder: Do you have a part that struggles to accept grace as an unearned, freely given gift?

J.O.Y.

Love the Lord your God with all your heart, with all your understanding and with all your strength, and to love your neighbor as yourself is more important than all burnt offerings and sacrifices. Mark 12:30-31

Have you ever heard of the acronym "JOY?" It stands for "Jesus, Others, You." One part of me loves the hierarchy but another part isn't so certain. According to JOY, we're supposed to put Jesus first, others after him, and ourselves last. But is that Biblical? When Jesus distilled the Ten Commandments, he told us, "Love the Lord your God with all your heart and with all your soul and with all your mind. This is the first and greatest commandment." So, yes, the Holy Triune God should always come first. But what about the next bit?

Jesus went on to say, "Love your neighbor as yourself." At first glance, it too seems to put neighbors (others) first. But does it really? The commandment states "as yourself." That indicates an equal measure of love for ourselves as for others. Not "first others, then yourself if there's anything left over."

Before we can love our neighbor, we have to understand what love is so it makes sense that after loving God, we have to love ourselves to know how or to even be able to love others.

We don't have to wait for the leftovers. *Love isn't limited.* Jesus told us to love God with everything we have got—heart, soul, mind. And when we do, we are filled up with everything we need. God is the source, the well, that gives life. Only when we have been filled—thus taking care of ourselves—can we have anything to give others. Putting God first is how we can be sure that we are taking care of ourselves *and* others.

Loving yourself isn't selfish. Loving *only* yourself would be.

Thoughts to ponder: Do you have a part that believes self-care is selfish? Does it believe that ignoring your own needs is more loving than tending to yourself first?

DIFFERENT PLACES ON THE PATH

"Will the Lord spurn forever, and never again be favorable? Has his steadfast love forever ceased? Are his promises at an end for all time? Has God forgotten to be gracious? Has he in anger shut up his compassion?" Then I said, "I will appeal to this: the years when the Most High stretched out his right hand." I will remember the deeds of the Lord; yes, I will remember your wonders of old. I will remember all your work, and meditate on your mighty deeds. Your way, O God, is holy. What God is great like our God? You are the God who works wonders; you have made known your might among the peoples. Psalm 77:7-14

Not all parts are in the same place in our spiritual journey. Some carry burdens that need healing, while others are snuggled right up in Jesus' lap. It can feel very strange to have faith in God's healing, yet still, be afraid of the illness. To fully trust that wherever God is leading is the absolute right path for you, but to be impatient with His timing. To crave connection of a church community but fear judgment from the critical and self-righteous. How can we have faith in one area but not in another?

When we consider that parts have different jobs and that some take on the responsibility for protecting us from different experiences, it makes a little more sense. Our parts have fears and/or emotional pain specific to their individual experiences. Two different parts will have two different opinions on what the "smart thing to do" is.

The most difficult question we will ever struggle with is "If God loves me, why does He let me suffer?" There is a part of me that is afraid I am too insignificant for God to care about. Or too unworthy.

I have a part who FREAKS OUT when my Doubting part speaks up. This part is afraid to not trust God. It's afraid of not being a "Good Christian." My "Must Have Faith" part is concerned about being ousted from God's good graces, but it is also concerned with not making God sad at my lack of faith. Unfortunately, this part's desire to shut down the Doubt is interfering with a direct, honest relationship with God. As soon as we hide feelings from ourselves and from God, we are like Adam and Eve hiding in the garden, hands and face sticky from eating illicit fruit. Parts that are driven by fear or who are consumed with rules and technicalities erect a barrier between parts and Self and between parts and God.

Self has an untainted, immutable relationship with the Godhead. Self is comfortable with the things it knows about God and the things that it doesn't. Self accepts mystery and majesty.

God already knows that we doubt. We're not fooling Him. He is not surprised by our flaws and failures. Jesus—like Self—yearns to comfort and heal our hurting, wounded, burdened parts. The Holy Spirit works and rests side by side with Self in the deep well of our hearts.

When we are in Self, we can open our hearts to the compassion and healing of the divine. In Self, we recognize the parts of ourselves that are hurting, the ones that are afraid, the ones that feel unworthy and we can hold these wounded little ones up to the divine Trinity, letting light and love heal the wrongs and evils that were done to them.

Thoughts to ponder: Do you have parts that try to hide from God? Do you have parts that you feel are unworthy of God's love?

I BELIEVE! KINDA

"IF I CAN?" SAID JESUS. "EVERYTHING
IS POSSIBLE FOR ONE WHO BELIEVES."
IMMEDIATELY THE BOY'S FATHER EXCLAIMED,
"I DO BELIEVE; HELP ME OVERCOME MY
UNBELIEF!" MARK 9:23-25

When the father of a young boy who was afflicted with convulsions brought his son to the disciples for healing, they were unable to do so. Can you imagine the parts that were likely triggered in the father by this disappointment? At some point, he must have heard about the miracles that Jesus was performing. He probably had a part that leaped with renewed hope. It's likely that he, the father, had tried other methods of prayer and healing and had watched them fail, so it wouldn't be surprising if he also had a part that was afraid to hope. Even still, this father's desperation to find healing for his boy made him seek out Jesus' group of wanderers.

The disciples attempted to heal the boy, unsuccessfully. While doing so, a crowd of irate teachers of the law gathered around them. An argument ensued.

I can only wonder what the father might have felt watching these two groups beef it out with each other. He needs help for his son. That's all he really cares about. He can't quite get to Jesus but instead is being "assisted" by his disciples who aren't making any headway and a bunch of angry lawyers start kicking up a fuss. How do you think Dad's Hope and Afraid-to-Hope parts were faring?

And then Jesus steps in! Once he gets caught up on the situation he turns to the father and says, "Bring me the boy." The boy is brought to Jesus and the spirit inside the boy freaks out and throws the kid around on the ground for a while. The father asks Jesus to take pity on them and, if he can, please help them.

Jesus says, "If I can? I can do anything if you believe in me."

Dad says, "Yes, I believe! But also, not so much."

He wasn't afraid to be completely honest with Jesus. He wanted to believe but he needed Jesus' help to get the whole way there. We need help even with our faith.

Jesus doesn't require a 100% No-Doubts-Allowed faith. He accepted the parts of the father that were struggling, and he healed the boy. He will accept yours, too.

Thoughts to ponder: How do you feel about the parts that doubt? Do you have other parts that try to control or shut down the doubting ones?

A HEART, DIVIDED

WHAT CAUSES FIGHTS AND QUARRELS AMONG YOU? DON'T THEY COME FROM YOUR DESIRES THAT BATTLE WITHIN YOU? COME NEAR TO GOD AND HE WILL COME NEAR TO YOU. WASH YOUR HANDS, YOU SINNERS, AND PURIFY YOUR HEARTS, YOU DOUBLE-MINDED. GRIEVE, MOURN, AND WAIL. CHANGE YOUR LAUGHTER TO MOURNING AND YOUR JOY TO GLOOM. JAMES 4:1, 9

There is a certain pain-filled limbo that exists in the space between two conflicting desires. James called it a "divided heart." Part of you wants one thing; another part is certain that the other thing is the best way to go. "Torn between two lovers," goes an old song. And it's no coincidence that "feelin' like a fool" is the next line.

Feeling caught between two choices, wavering and fretting over what to do, certain one minute and filled with doubt the next—this pendulum swing of non-decision makes a person feel weak and, indeed, foolish.

Sometimes this indecision occurs when parts have different agendas. For example, one part might value the safety of the familiar regardless of unpleasant (or even abusive) circumstances while another part is ready to take the risk of leaving because its job involves being assertive. These two well-meaning parts create a deadlock that leaves us stuck and confused at our seeming inability to make a decision.

And when we try to use logic to force a decision, we come up against an implacable wall of emotion. Deep down, we know what we *should* do but our parts keep us frozen "for our own good."

We can spend a lot of time doing Pro and Con lists, getting advice, and mulling over the options until 3:00 in the morning as we lie in the dark, mind racing, wishing we could sleep. But unless we take the time to listen—really listen—to the parts involved in the deadlock we will remain stuck. Parts do not give up. Ever. At some particularly difficult time in our past, their lives—our lives—depended on them dealing with a problem in a certain, specific kind of way. They learned their lesson well.

Unless we can help each part feel heard and feel safe enough to relax their holds on what they see as The One True Way, we will stay stuck.

Stop fighting. Listen.

Thoughts to ponder: What parts have been at war within you recently? Take time with each one, to understand their point of view. How did they acquire that particular opinion or belief in the rightness of their own way? Why was it so important? What is each one afraid of now, if they don't get their way?

DIRECT ACCESS

AND I HEARD A LOUD VOICE FROM THE THRONE SAYING, "LOOK! GOD'S DWELLING PLACE IS NOW AMONG THE PEOPLE, AND HE WILL DWELL WITH THEM. THEY WILL BE HIS PEOPLE, AND GOD HIMSELF WILL BE WITH THEM AND BE THEIR GOD. REV 21:3

In Internal Family Systems, there is a technique called "direct access," which is when the therapist communicates directly with a client's parts. So instead of asking the client to turn inward to talk with a part, the clinician will simply go right to the source and speak directly to a member of the client's Inner World.

God also gives us direct access to him. He sent his son, Jesus, to reside on earth with us. God did not do this because he needed to learn what it was like to be human. It certainly wasn't for his benefit. God sent Jesus and thereafter, the Holy Spirit so that we can be restored to Their presence. Immanuel means "God is with us" and that is not possible without Jesus' sacrifice which absorbed our sins.

God: the Supreme Creator of the universe

Is: present tense of "be"

With: a function word signifying connection and agreement

Us: you and me

Through prayer and the intercession of the Holy Spirit, we have the same kind of direct access to God. When we don't know how or even what to pray, the Holy Spirit does. Romans 8:26-27 says, "In the same way, the Spirit helps us in our weakness. We do not know what we ought to pray for, but the Spirit himself intercedes for us through wordless groans. And he who searches our hearts knows the mind of the Spirit because the Spirit intercedes for God's people in accordance with the will of God."

There are times when our prayers may seem empty or futile, but we are not alone in them. When our pain is too deep for words to express, the Spirit moves in our hearts and groans to the Creator *on our behalf.* We suffer together. We are not alone.

Thoughts to ponder: What do you think about a Supreme Holy Being who decided the only way to be with us was to come for us Himself? How can you benefit from this generosity? How can you increase your direct access to God?

THE DARK

Finally, be strong in the Lord and in his mighty power. Put on the full armor of God, so that you can take your stand against the devil's schemes. For our struggle is not against flesh and blood, but against the rulers, against the authorities, against the powers of this dark world and against the spiritual forces of evil in the heavenly realms. Eph 6: 10-12

Some Christians try to ignore the existence of Satan. But if there is light, there is dark. The Bible is clear that demons exist and that we are at war with them. In Internal Family Systems, these dark spiritual entities are called "unattached burdens." They are recognizable as dark energy, otherworldly negative entities that can pollute our spirits and which must be dealt with in order to heal and find peace.

These are not parts we are born with but may have acquired through choices we may have made. We may have unknowingly invited these dark spirits into our psyche. Sin is their entry point. Bitterness, unforgiveness, selfishness, etc. are what feed the critters. These negative energies may also be aspects of the burdens that certain traumatized and wounded parts carry.

But what about "All parts are welcome?" Excellent question. Yes, all parts really are welcome because they are us as God created us to be. Again, these dark entities are not born in us. They are unattached, foreign, dark spirits. They don't belong to us and, more importantly, we don't belong to them.

Jesus knew how to handle demons. He cast them out. Furthermore, he taught and gave authority to his disciples to do so as well.

When we seek healing and the "renewal of [our] mind" through Christ, sin is ousted and we are free to be all that God has designed us for—"good, pleasing, and [conforming to] the perfect will of God."

Dark spirits are tricky. There are times when it is a good idea to seek help. You may need to summon up your courage and reach out to someone who has been gifted with the discernment to recognize and distinguish between spirits. Spiritual warfare isn't meant to be battled all on our own.

Thoughts to ponder: What are your opinions about Satan and demons? Are there points in your past where you may have been exposed to evil?

STUCK & CONFUSED

FOR WE KNOW THAT THE LAW IS SPIRITUAL, BUT I AM OF THE FLESH, SOLD UNDER SIN. FOR I DO NOT UNDERSTAND MY OWN ACTIONS. FOR I DO NOT DO WHAT I WANT, BUT I DO THE VERY THING I HATE. NOW IF I DO WHAT I DO NOT WANT, I AGREE WITH THE LAW, THAT IT IS GOOD. SO NOW IT IS NO LONGER I WHO DO IT, BUT SIN THAT DWELLS WITHIN ME. FOR I KNOW THAT NOTHING GOOD DWELLS IN ME, THAT IS, IN MY FLESH. FOR I HAVE THE DESIRE TO DO WHAT IS RIGHT, BUT NOT THE ABILITY TO CARRY IT OUT. FOR I DO NOT DO THE GOOD I WANT, BUT THE EVIL I DO NOT WANT IS WHAT I KEEP ON DOING. NOW IF I DO WHAT I DO NOT WANT, IT IS NO LONGER I WHO DO IT, BUT SIN THAT DWELLS WITHIN ME. SO, I FIND IT TO BE A LAW THAT WHEN I WANT TO DO RIGHT, EVIL LIES CLOSE AT HAND. FOR I DELIGHT IN THE LAW OF GOD, IN MY INNER BEING, BUT I SEE IN MY MEMBERS ANOTHER LAW WAGING WAR AGAINST THE LAW OF MY MIND AND

> MAKING ME CAPTIVE TO THE LAW OF SIN THAT DWELLS IN MY MEMBERS. WRETCHED MAN THAT I AM! WHO WILL DELIVER ME FROM THIS BODY OF DEATH? THANKS BE TO GOD THROUGH JESUS CHRIST OUR LORD! SO THEN, I MYSELF SERVE THE LAW OF GOD WITH MY MIND, BUT WITH MY FLESH I SERVE THE LAW OF SIN. ROM 7: 14-25

There were times when even Paul didn't understand himself. In Romans 7:14-20, Paul describes his utter bewilderment with the internal conflict of knowing what he should do and yet not doing it. Knowing his childhood background, it makes sense to me that Paul might have struggled with some legalistic parts. He grew up with a lot of "shoulds" and "don'ts."

But after miraculously meeting Jesus, Paul became led by the Holy Spirit. Paul seemed pretty in touch with his Self and the Spirit yet even he experienced the inner conflict of not measuring up to his own expectations. Paul was human after all, and no human aside from Christ Jesus could ever be perfect and without sin.

"I do not understand what I do. For what I want to do I do not do, but what I hate I do."

Boy, can I relate! I don't want to eat the potato chips, but I do. I want to exercise, but I don't. I don't want to take my end-of-a-long-day frustrations out on my family, but I do.

I am not always who I want to be.

That can be confusing as well as shame-inducing.

Paul writes that he wants to do good, but he just can't quite manage it. In Paul's "innermost being [he] delights in God's law." Paul's Self delights. But Paul also sees "another law at work" deep within himself. Another part of him is waging war against his desires (to do good), making him feel wretched, trapped, and confused at his weaknesses.

Yet Paul knows where to look for rescue. "Thanks be to God, who delivers me through Jesus Christ our Lord."

Thoughts to ponder: When was the most recent time that you have felt stuck and confused by your own choices? What parts might have been involved?

LEAVES THE NINETY-NINE

"SEE THAT YOU DO NOT DESPISE ONE OF THESE LITTLE ONES. FOR I TELL YOU THAT IN HEAVEN THEIR ANGELS ALWAYS SEE THE FACE OF MY FATHER WHO IS IN HEAVEN. WHAT DO YOU THINK? IF A MAN HAS A HUNDRED SHEEP, AND ONE OF THEM HAS GONE ASTRAY, DOES HE NOT LEAVE THE NINETY-NINE ON THE MOUNTAINS AND GO IN SEARCH OF THE ONE THAT WENT ASTRAY? AND IF HE FINDS IT, TRULY, I SAY TO YOU, HE REJOICES OVER IT MORE THAN OVER THE NINETY-NINE THAT NEVER WENT ASTRAY. SO IT IS NOT THE WILL OF MY FATHER WHO IS IN HEAVEN THAT ONE OF THESE LITTLE ONES SHOULD PERISH. MATT 18: 10-14

Jesus delighted in searching out and rescuing the lost, the "unworthy," the untouchables—the exiles, in fact. He was born into an age and culture that rigidly confined people to specific roles and rules and specific spheres in society. But he didn't bother with all that. That's one reason he infuriated the religious leaders. They howled with anger whenever Jesus brushed aside the segregated class system.

Jesus loves the lost and the wounded. He came for us—for you and me. He and the angels all celebrate when a soul is brought back to the fold. When we think about Jesus' love for the lost, we often think in terms of evangelism—reaching out to bring other people into the light of Christ. But what about ourselves? What about our own untouchables?

Is there a part of you that resists accepting the forgiveness of Christ? Sometimes these militant parts believe that if they relax even a little bit we will fall into laziness or embarrass ourselves in some way. Sometimes refusing to show mercy to ourselves comes from the belief that we are unworthy of comfort or love.

When we hate and reject parts of ourselves, we are rejecting an aspect of God's creation. We are ignoring the trauma, the hurts, and the wounds that placed immeasurable burdens on these Littles. How would your wounded parts feel if, instead of rejection, you offered grace? Instead of criticism, love? Instead of punishment, mercy?

Thoughts to ponder: Explore what parts might be withholding grace and mercy. Seek to understand their fears and concerns.

CIVIL WAR

WHAT CAUSES FIGHTS AND QUARRELS AMONG YOU? DON'T THEY COME FROM THE BATTLE WITHIN? JAMES 4:1

For many people, quarrels create as much or more internal conflict as external. If something occurs where a boundary has to be set, a lot of internal conflict gets stirred up before we even get to the actual quarrel. That internal conflict involves parts with different needs, fears, beliefs, and agendas.

Here's an example:

Something is said that stings a wounded part.

Exile: I can't believe he just said that. [The body flushes with embarrassment and sadness at not being understood.]

Angry Manager: Does he think I'm stupid? I've been doing this job for X number of years without anyone's help. Where does he get off? I should say something. [Tension builds in the neck, shoulders, and head.]

Fearful Manager: I should say something? Really? Is it worth it? I mean, what if I misunderstood? Maybe he thought he was helping? [Stomach is queasy.]

A Walled Off Manager: After what he just said? Not likely. I'm not going to trust him with that other project I was thinking about. [Walks off in a huff.]

Inner Brooder: I don't have to deal with this. [Grows irritable and isolative. In the ensuing hours, we come up with multiple imaginary scenarios in which we slay our opponent with our biting and scintillating wit.]

Disordered-Eater Firefighter: I need chocolate. Lots of chocolate. [Nom nom nom!]

Shame (Protector): I'm so stupid. I should have said something. Why don't I ever stand up for myself? And on top of it, I blew my diet! I suck! [Stays in a bad mood for the rest of the day.]

As you can see, conflict can stir up a lot of parts. Frankly, we don't even need another person around to start the Civil War in our own heads. Any insomniac can vouch for that.

How do we calm this battle within? By taking the time to understand our parts and allowing the Spirit-led Self to bring healing to the system. In the example above we could choose to start with the part of us that got instantly angry, the part that was afraid to set a boundary, the part that dreamed about righting the scales of injustice and proving our intelligence, the part that sought comfort through sugar or carbs, the part that weaponizes shame in an attempt to control future behaviors, or underneath it all, the part that has been deeply hurt in the past by someone whose treatment of us taught us to believe that we are not good enough.

Thoughts to ponder: Have you felt like there is a battle going on inside? Which parts were involved?

SPIRITUAL MANAGERS

Then Jesus said to the crowds and to his disciples, "The scribes and the Pharisees sit on Moses' seat, so do and observe whatever they tell you, but not the works they do. For they preach, but do not practice. They tie up heavy burdens, hard to bear, and lay them on people's shoulders, but they themselves are not willing to move them with their finger. They do all their deeds to be seen by others.   Matt 23:1-5

Read the Bible. Pray. Go to church. Serve. Join. Do your daily devotions. Keep the Sabbath. Forgive others. Repent. Meditate.

These are the Christian "shoulds"—the things we should do to be better people. Better Christ-followers. I'm sure you can think of plenty more, especially if we go secular: exercise, diet, self-care. Find a work/life balance. Drink your water. And so on...

These are all very, very good things. But when we practice them out of a sense of forced obligation and/or to evade anxiety or avoid negative feelings by taking a shortcut past feeling difficult emotions, then we are probably allowing our managers free reign. In general, managers like rules so it makes sense that they might lean more heavily on the Law than on the Spirit. Managers crave clarity. As we try hard to please God with our efforts to follow Christ, it can be difficult to remember that it isn't our efforts that really matter. It's the heart behind them that makes all the difference.

The Pharisees were a group of devout religious leaders who had frequent run-ins with Jesus. He seemed to both attract and repel them. At the time, the Pharisees were men who had dedicated their lives to studying and observing every detail of Judaic law—presumably to please God. That's the good part.

Unfortunately, the Pharisees turned their status into a rigid judgmental brotherhood. They believed they were better than the laypeople. They got caught up in the rules and the Law and lost sight of who it was all for. That's not good.

When Christian practices are used to avoid feeling our emotions then we are corrupting the very disciplines that are supposed to be guiding us in deepening our faith and connection to the Most Holy.

Thoughts to ponder: How do you know if you are doing these things (praying, reading the Bible, serving at church, etc.) for the right reasons?

WEARY & BURDENED

COME TO ME, ALL WHO ARE WEARY AND
BURDENED, AND I WILL GIVE YOU REST. MATT
11:28

Managers are exhausted. They are relentless, ever vigilant, dedicated helpers. They have a mission. They must not fail. And this mission, whatever it is, was essential to your physical and/or emotional survival. That's why the part pledged itself to the mission in the first place. To save you.

It's been a 24/7/365 work shift for however many years these parts have been doing their job. No sick days. No breaks. No vacation. No reprieve. No rest.

Matthew 11:28 says "Come to me, all who are weary and burdened, and I will give you rest."

Wouldn't that be amazing? That rest is there for all of us, including our wearied parts. But to truly rest in Jesus we have to have access to our Self. When parts are burdened and/or activated, they eclipse our Self. Self is there. It's just in the background because parts are busily doing what parts do. Burdened parts are incapable of relaxing from their mission until they learn to trust Self.

Thoughts to ponder: Are your parts tired? Are they ready to accept the rest that Jesus offers?

JESUS WEPT

Now when Mary came to where Jesus was and saw him, she fell at his feet, saying to him, "Lord, if you had been here, my brother would not have died." When Jesus saw her weeping, and the Jews who had come with her also weeping, he was deeply moved in his spirit and greatly troubled. And he said, "Where have you laid him?" They said to him, "Lord, come and see." Jesus wept. So, the Jews said, "See how he loved him!" But some of them said, "Could not he who opened the eyes of the blind man also have kept this man from dying?" Then Jesus, deeply moved again, came to the tomb. It was a cave, and a stone lay against it. Jesus said, "Take away the stone." Martha, the sister of the dead man, said to him, "Lord, by this time there will be an odor, for he has been dead four days." Jesus said to her, "Did I not tell you that if

YOU BELIEVED YOU WOULD SEE THE GLORY OF GOD?" JOHN 11: 32-40

We run away from pain. It's a natural instinct to move away from physical pain such as jerking your hand off of a hot stovetop. Likewise, we react with similar instinctive aversion to emotional, mental, or spiritual pain. It's not uncommon to want to run away from others' pain, too.

Jesus didn't run. When his good friend Lazarus died, Jesus went to Lazarus' sisters, Mary and Martha. He spent time with each of them, listening and comforting. When he saw how sad Lazarus' friends and family were, Jesus was moved by their anguish and wept with them even though Jesus knew that he was going to fix it by raising Lazarus from the dead. Jesus had been aware that he was going to perform a miracle for several days before he even got to Lazarus' home. He knew he was going to bring great joy. But Jesus didn't rush past the pain—theirs or his own. He felt it. He allowed himself and those around him to experience the terrible loss.

Jesus must also have known that his death wasn't that far away, and he knew it wasn't going to be an easy one. This reminder of the torture he would be subjected to and of his own mortality would have been excruciatingly painful. Even though, once again, Jesus knew he would overcome death—both Lazarus' and his own—Jesus allowed himself to be fully immersed in the grief rather than simply sweeping the experience. He suffered and he allowed others to suffer.

Thoughts to ponder: What parts do you have that get activated by pain—either emotional or physical? Are there times you have wished that Jesus would just sweep it aside for you? Why do you think Jesus allowed himself and others to grieve Lazarus' death?

WASTE NOT

AND WE KNOW THAT GOD WORKS TOGETHER ALL THINGS FOR GOOD FOR THOSE WHO LOVE HIM, FOR THOSE WHO ARE CALLED ACCORDING TO PURPOSE. ROMANS 8:28

Suffering can be confusing. As if the pain isn't bad enough, we often get tangled up in assigning blame. Strangely, if we can blame someone, including ourselves, for the suffering in a particular situation, we are often able to accept the situation more easily. Likewise, when suffering is a direct consequence of choices we have made, we tend not to feel abandoned by God. But when bad things happen for no apparent good reason, we may find ourselves asking God the eternal question "Why?"

Why did you let this happen, God?

Why did you do this to me?

Why won't you help?

Sometimes when we are in a suffering season other Christians can be rather unhelpful. They might ask us to examine our hearts for sin. That's not bad advice but not all suffering is a direct consequence of sin. That "It must be something you did" advice has a shaming quality to it that can be difficult to accept, especially when we are already hurting. My guess is these pious folks feel more comfortable believing that there is some way to control suffering. That is, by not sinning. They equate being good with being blessed and being bad with being punished. And sometimes that's true. But we can't control God with our actions.

Other friends might point out that we have the opportunity to grow from suffering. That is also true. Does that mean that God is inflicting us with pain so that our faith can grow? Seems kind of harsh. But again, God is God. Sometimes we *are* being tested. Sometimes the pain is used to foster greater dependence on God and to lead us to a more Christ-like connection with God.

Christ suffered. So will we. The truth is that sometimes we just don't know why things happen the way they do. But God does.

Thoughts to ponder: The places we have some control during these seasons of suffering are:

1) Do we declare God's sovereignty and seek His comfort in the midst of our pain, and

2) Do we allow God to use the suffering to mold our hearts—and heal our parts—to His will?

BOOKS AND WORKBOOKS

Anderson, Frank. *Transcending Trauma: Healing Complex PTSD with Internal Family Systems Therapy*. Eau Claire WI: PESI Publishing, 2021.

Earley, Jay. *Self-Therapy: A Step-By-Step Guide to Creating Wholeness and Healing Your Inner Child Using IFS*. Larkspur, CA: Pattern System Books, 2010.

Glass, Michelle. *Daily Parts Meditation Practice™: A Journey of Embodied Integration for Clients and Therapists*. Eugene, OR: Listen3r, 2016.

Peyton, Sarah. *Your Resonant Self: Guided Meditations and Exercises to Engage Your Brain's Capacity for Healing*. New York, NY: W.W. Norton & Co, 2017.

Riesmersma, Jenna. *Altogether You: Experiencing personal and spiritual transformation with Internal Family Systems therapy*. Marietta, GA: Pivotal Press, 2020.

Schwartz, Richard C. *No Bad Parts: Healing Trauma & Restoring Wholeness with the Internal Family Systems Model*. Boulder CO: Sounds True Publishing, 2021.

___. *Introduction to the Internal Family Systems Model*. Oak Park, IL: Trailheads Publications, 2001.

____. *You Are the One You've Been Waiting For: Bringing Courageous Love to Intimate Relationships.* Oak Park, IL: Trailheads Publishing, 2008.

Steege, Mary. *The Spirit-Lead Life: A Christian Encounter with Internal Family Systems.* Racine, WI: 2010

Weiss Bonnie. *Self-Therapy Workbook: An Exercise Book for the IFS Process.* Larkspur, CA: Pattern System Books, 2013.

ABOUT THE AUTHOR

Donna Glaser is a Licensed Professional Counselor in WI, IL, and MI; an Internal Family Systems-informed therapist; a Certified Anxiety Treatment Professional (CATP) and a Certified Complex Trauma Professional (CCTP-II) and author who lives in northwestern Wisconsin. Her favorite quote is by Oscar Wilde: "The final mystery is oneself." It seems to cover facets of both careers—psychotherapy as well as writing. All of her passions deal with relationships and exploring the past to gain a deeper understanding—and, perhaps, better control of—the present. She is also the author of the Letty Whittaker 12-Step Mystery and the Blood Visions Paranormal Mystery series.

Also By

Donna's books can be found on Amazon on her Author Page:
Donna White Glaser

FICTION

The Letty Whittaker 12-Step Mystery Series:

THE ENEMY WE KNOW

THE ONE WE LOVE

THE SECRETS WE KEEP

THE BLOOD WE SPILL

THE LIES WE TELL

The Blood Visions Paranormal Mystery Series:

A SCRYING SHAME

SCRY ME A RIVER

Made in the USA
Monee, IL
25 June 2022

98589872R00111